COPING WITH JOB
STRESS

A GUIDE FOR EMPLOYERS & EMPLOYEES

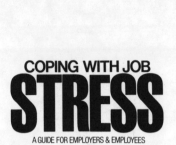

Herbert Greenberg, Ph. D., is the founder of Stress Management, Carlsbad, California and conducts workshops and seminars on stress management. He is also the author of *Teaching With Feeling* and *To Educate With Love.*

COPING WITH JOB
STRESS

A GUIDE FOR EMPLOYERS & EMPLOYEES

PRENTICE HALL PRESS • NEW YORK

Published in 1986 by Prentice Hall Press
A Division of Simon & Schuster, Inc.
Gulf + Western Building
One Gulf + Western Plaza
New York, NY 10023

Originally published by Prentice-Hall, Inc.
Design and production by York Graphic Services, Inc.,
York, Pennsylvania 17404
PRENTICE HALL PRESS is a trademark of Simon & Schuster, Inc.

Library of Congress Cataloging-in-Publication Data
Greenberg, Herbert M.
Coping with job stress.
Includes index.
1. Job stress.   I. Title.
HF5548.85.G73   158.7   80-11330
ISBN 0-13-172403-7 (pbk.)

Manufactured in the United States of America

15   14   13   12   11   10   9

CONTENTS

Preface   vii
Special Note to the Reader   x
Introduction—Why Change?   1

Part One—Telling It Like It Is   **5**
1. Our Aching Bodies   7
2. Unreasonable Behaviors   16
3. Anger Situations   23
4. Dumping Stress On Our Families   35
5. Is My Stress Level Too High?   39
6. Don't Trust Your Feelings   51

Part Two—Breaking The Pattern   **59**
7. Don't Talk—Walk!   61
8. The Do-Nut—Kicking the Anger Habit   78
9. Talking to Others   89
10. Slow Down   97
11. Crises and Emergencies   106
12. Muscle Relaxation Methods   114
13. Pleasurable Goodies   126

14. Support Groups 142
15. Human Pain 146

Part Three—Taking Care of Yourself **153**
16. Guilt 155
17. Solitude 161
18. The Me-Act 171
19. Physical Health 182
20. The Competitive Challenge 189
21. Sex 197

Part Four—Can I Really Change? **203**
22. Personal Strengths 205
23. Stop Indulging Your Feelings 214
24. A Code of Behavior 223
25. Diversify Your Emotions 229
26. Cop-Outs, Excuses, and Rationalizations 234

Part Five—Putting It All Together **237**
27. Recall Aids 239
28. Your Own Unique Pattern 247
Epilogue 249
Appendix—Recall Reminders 253
References and Further Reading 260

PREFACE

Job stress is no longer considered the sole prerogative of the top executive or the busy air controller. We now recognize that all work requires stress, that all jobs produce stress.

And significant as work is in our lives, it is far from the sole contributor to our total stress load. Being married or having a partner inevitably adds to our stress. Parenthood boosts the stress load considerably higher, and single parents and working mothers feel an even heavier burden. Any involvement you have in your community, school, or church adds more stress to your life.

The broader political and international world we live in also adds to our stress load. It does this whenever it touches us personally (as in the gasoline crisis) but also indirectly through our daily exposure to the violence and blast of the media. And to all these externally imposed stressors, we add our own self-determined ones: inner expectations, high personal standards, demands on our selves. Stress mounts even higher.

With all these sources of stress, its no wonder more people are asking themselves: "How do I know if my stress level is harmful or too high?" "How can I keep my stress under control?" "What are the options in handling pressures, responsibilities?"

Some years ago, soon after my father died of his third heart attack, I began to raise these questions for myself. I began to look seriously at my own behaviors, my total life style. I was clearly a coronary-prone individual (Rosenman & Friedman, 1974). I had many of the bad traits, many of the poor habits.

At first, my motivation was intensely personal. I wanted to avoid heart disease, to enjoy life more, to change some undesirable behaviors, and, I hoped, to live longer. I went to work on myself. But with twenty-five years of experience in helping others to change, my motivation (and excitement) quickly spilled over into my professional life. I soon found myself reading all I could about stress, learning about it, teaching others about it.

This book is an attempt to summarize both my personal search (which continues to this day) as well as the much broader search of the hundreds of individuals who sought answers with me—individuals from many occupations and professions, from varying work situations.

What has emerged is a wide range of techniques that are useful for varied personalities and life styles, that are applicable to diverse occupations and work situations.

The material is organized in five parts. The first part helps us to recognize our stress level with special *self-monitoring* tools. Our feelings, total behaviors, and body data are considered in depth. A central theme emphasizes that higher levels of stress result (in all of us) in irrational, unreasonable behavior and in lowered job productivity as well.

Part Two, the *basic technique* section, offers a wide variety of techniques to lower stress to more reasonable and productive levels. A large number of options are offered to suit each individual—his or her unique personality, job station, and situation. Anger and job dissatisfaction are considered in depth, as well as special tools for coming to grips with typical work situations.

Part Three focuses on a recurring reaction typical of many of us under stress—neglecting the *care of oneself*. Under pressure most individuals remain responsibly dedicated to their work but become irresponsibly neglectful of themselves. Our needs for total renewal—for care of our emotions, our mental condition, and our physical state are all considered in depth.

Parts Four and Five focus on *self-discipline* and *personal application* of the techniques. Changing lifelong, ingrained mechanisms may not be easy. Special techniques are considered; attitudes are explored and discussed. A special feature are the Recall Reminders, which assist the reader to apply consistently the techniques offered in this book. Special emphases on developing a personalized program for change and on maintaining change are part of these sections.

A good deal of this book is the contribution of others, primarily those who have attended my seminars and courses. I am continually impressed by the creative and unique ways different individuals interpret what I have to offer, adapt it, and integrate it into their lives. This book greatly reflects these contributions.

Many persons have enriched my own ways of looking at stress. For their obvious influence, I want to thank Chuck Clark, Mike Runyon, Dave Pascoe, Gary Yeatts, Bob Satterlee, Ellen Abbott, and Dennis Naiman. Also: Carl Lee of the California Highway Patrol, Jim Post of Xerox Corporation, Ron Hochwalt of the San Diego County Department of Education, and many, many more.

Most of all, my thanks to my loving and patient wife. I owe her a great deal, and to her this book, in its entirety, is hereby dedicated.

SPECIAL NOTE
TO THE READER

If you were attending a seminar on job stress, you would probably take notes on any comments or ideas that struck you personally or rung a bell. You would undoubtedly jot down techniques you would want to remember. You would probably note for yourself just how you would apply these techniques to your own unique job situation and life style.

You can make similar notes to yourself while reading this book. You can make mental notes, but many of you will probably find written notes more useful and more available when you need them (while under high stress!). The Recall Reminders at the end of each chapter provide you with the opportunity to do just that—to make notes for yourself on the content of each chapter.

If you prefer not writing in the book, then turn to page 253 in the Appendix, where all the Recall Reminders for the entire book are collected chapter by chapter in one place. Take those eight pages to any copy machine, and you will have the entire book summarized for you.

As you write your notes on these three summary pages, you will then have a personalized set of notes for yourself. Individuals have found these notes tremendously useful in helping them to develop their own personal plan for stress management. They are also well tested as a means for you to recall alternatives and options for handling your own stress (see Chapter 27 for specific suggestions.).

COPING WITH JOB
STRESS
A GUIDE FOR EMPLOYERS & EMPLOYEES

INTRODUCTION— WHY CHANGE?

Jack performs well under stress. He's excited by stress, stimulated by it. He feels especially alive in highly stressed situations. He may be an elected official, a salesman, a competitive athlete, a schoool administrator. He likes deadlines; he likes others coming to him with problems to solve. He seems to thrive on competition and challenges. He's successful, and he wouldn't consider any other kind of work. And yet he has difficulty turning it off. He's wondering about the value of slowing his life down—of spending more time fishing, on relaxing hobbies, or just with his family. He'd like to develop, at times at least, a slower pace. He'd like to learn a new style of living to add to his comfortable and successful life. Jack wants to learn more about stress.

Joan is conscientious and competent. She may be a bookkeeper, a mathematical analyst, an executive secretary. She is well recognized by her fellow employees and her supervisor. She often feels tugged from many different directions; she feels splintered—at times, even overwhelmed. She doesn't find it easy to say no; she takes on a great deal but always manages to accomplish it successfully. At times, however, the cost seems high. She doesn't have time to enjoy herself; she says it's difficult to relax; she would like to find ways to unwind a little. She feels those tension headaches after a tough day that often ruin her evenings. Joan wants to learn new ways to cope with her job stress.

Art is a work-a-holic; he can't stop working on tasks, projects, and jobs. He might be a sales representative, a repair man, a trouble-shooter, an accountant. He says he needs pressures, deadlines, and responsibility in order to get things done. But even when the outside demands stop, he can't stop. He then creates his own pressures. At home, he seeks out things to do, projects to begin, problems that need solving. He can't slow down. He can't relax. He drives his secretary crazy; his subordinates can't keep up with him. His wife loves him but doesn't find it easy living with him. People at work think he's a candidate for a heart attack, and his wife's worried, too. He's beginning, at times, to wonder if it's worth it. He'd like to sleep better; he says he doesn't know how to relax. Art's obviously experiencing stress. He wants to change.

Joe may be an engineer, a production worker, a sales manager, or the boss of a small retail establishment. He is proud of his Mediterranean heritage; he believes in letting his feelings out. "I don't have stress; I give it to others," he says. He sure does. If criticized by the boss or a customer, he is angry and complaining all day. He dumps it on his fellow workers or subordinates. He ridicules his wife and puts down the kids. He seems to enjoy being angry. But lately the feedback from his coworkers, wife, and children is beginning to get to him. He wants to learn ways to control his emotions, to be less excitable, to feel less guilty. He too is experiencing stress. He would like to be angry less often. Joe's ready to change.

Bob enjoys his work. He is a lifetime career person. He could be a lawyer, a manager in law enforcement, an executive in production. He has a quiet manner and is generally calm, deliberate, and competent. He feels that he handles most situations pretty well, but he recognizes that others react differently than he. He'd like to know how he fits in with everyone else. He's curious about stress. He'd like to appreciate some of his more emotional subordinates better; he'd like to understand his wife more than he does. He asks, "Am I possibly a 'stress carrier'? Am I causing stress in others?" He's curious, interested, and open; he too wants to learn more about stress.

Evelyn is a perfectionist. She could be a clerical supervisor, a head nurse, a school teacher, or a government office employee. When she gets annoyed at subordinates or co-workers, she keeps most of it inside. It builds up, and she frequently gets physical symptoms that bother her. She says, "I am a worrier and the most impatient person I know." She hates waiting in lines, likes to drive fast, and doesn't like others to slow her down or block her. She realizes that her stress is self-imposed. She would like to worry less, sleep more, become more tolerant of others, and not take things so seriously. Evelyn would like to find some new ways of dealing with the stress in her life.

Dick's a manager and quite successful in his career. He could be anywhere in private industry, in government, in educational administration, or in law enforcement. He keeps it together well. At work, he's sensitive to his subordinates and is well liked. He stays cool and doesn't get up tight. He meets deadlines and gets things done. He realizes that he takes a lot of it home, that he's not always pleasant to be with. He needs to unwind alone. He doesn't feel like relating to his wife or kids. He'd rather watch TV, read, or retreat to his workshop. He enjoys one or two drinks, and he smokes a pack or two a day. He worries about his health and would like to give up smoking. His father died at forty-four of a sudden heart attack. Someone at the office recently had a stroke. Dick's doctor gives him a clean bill of health. Dick's still scared. "Will it happen to me?" He'd like to recognize what, if anything, is happening to him. "Am I coping adequately with stress?" he wants to know.

Tom was recently promoted to supervisor. He might

work in a bank, a supermarket, a production line, or a drafting firm. Supervising others is a new responsibility for him. His subordinates come to him with crises, problems, and complaints. He feels that he must always be available and that he must know how to handle every problem that arises. He's not always sure he handles things well. He says, "I keep cool but don't feel that way inside." He'd like to "learn to handle the pressure." Tom's certainly ready to learn new ways of coping with job stress.

These people are not job failures or misfits. They are not problem employees. These are normal people. They are mostly successful in their careers. They are competent individuals. Their productivity is well recognized in their work situations. Any one of them could be the man or woman working in the office next to yours or in the job alongside you. They could even be you.

These people and hundreds like them have attended special workshops set up so that individuals can learn more about job stress and the many alternative ways of coping with it. That's what this book is all about.

TELLING IT LIKE IT IS

1

OUR ACHING BODIES

Walt didn't sleep so well last night. And when he awoke, he felt tired, less energetic in facing his day. And the day didn't start out too well either. His toast burned, the kids made a lot of noise at breakfast, and he was glad to get out of the house. But there was a traffic tie-up on the way to work. He got there late and had to park in the far parking lot. To top it off, someone "joked" about his coming in late. He tried to become engrossed in his work but was interrupted by unimportant telephone calls; by a complaint from a co-worker; and, later, by mild criticism from a superior. Things seemed to go on like this all day. A deadline was moved up for production; another report was due. Walt felt tense and tight all day long. He tried, however, to act friendly with coworkers and customers. Walt, like many of us, wanted to appear calm, cool, and in control of things. By the time he arrived home that evening he felt tired, tense, and weary. And he had that aching pain in his shoulders and neck that he gets after a particularly tough day.

Walt had been experiencing stress all day—keeping it inside, building it up. His stress finally accumulated where it often does for him. He had a real "pain in the neck."

Our bodies are important sources of information regarding our stress level. Building up stress all day may affect you (as it does Walt) in the neck, or the pain could be in your head or in your lower back. It may hit your digestive system or somewhere on your skin. It might be your rising blood pressure or some symptom of coronary heart disease—wherever that particular place is in your body that collects all the stress that accumulates all day.

Much has been written and probably even more has been said about the effects of stress/emotion on our body and on our health. Although occasionally some of the claims are extreme and at times even unsupported by sound research, this should in no way confuse the basic fact: *Stress can cause or seriously aggravate a variety of body problems and illnesses.* This statement is substantiated by extensive research in the fields of physiology and medicine and by years of experience by well-respected practitioners in all fields of physical health and psychology.

I will briefly summarize several areas where this has been well documented and supported. This should suffice to increase your awareness of the bodily effects of stress. You can then apply this mind/body concept to your own body.

First, let us look at *the fields of psychosomatic medicine and research*. The awareness of the psychic causation of illness goes back to antiquity, but in the 1930s serious scientific study began to lend further support to this basic idea. Since then, a tremendous amount of evidence has accumulated in support of the emotional causation of a host of diseases and bodily impairments (Arieti, 1975). In more recent years, the word stress has been used to describe this emotional or psychological causation. Investigators have studied a wide variety of illnesses, ranging from asthma and skin rashes to arthritis and even to cancer. In addition to the practitioner fields, there has been extensive research in actually producing specific body illnesses experimentally. Some of the better known classic experiments were with monkeys. Ulcers were actually experimentally induced in monkeys when they were placed in stress situations made as similar as possible to certain stresses of human executives. These studies proved beyond a doubt that emotions can cause body illness. The monkeys used in these experiments were of course labeled "executive" monkeys (Brady, 1967; Weiss, 1975). As a consequence of psychosomatic medicine and research, there should be no serious question in the reader's mind that real physical changes can be caused in our bodies—not just by viruses, bacteria, or other "bugs" but also by our emotions and the stress induced by them.

A second area of extensive research is the study of *life changes*. The idea that changes in our life situations, particularly crises, makes us more susceptible to illness is also an idea with roots deeply embedded in the past. In the 1960s, however, two researchers, Rahe and Holmes, lent considerable sophistication to previous studies into life changes. They developed a scale that quantified life change events in terms of their likelihood of producing symptoms of illness. Extensive research by many individuals for almost twenty years has developed this concept considerably (Rahe & Arthur, 1978). A copy of the scale is provided in Figure 1–1. Note that all our life change events add to our chances of getting physically sick. Even such "positive" experiences as marriage, vacations, outstanding personal achievements, and the like add to our susceptibility to illness. The extensive studies that have been done all add up to the same conclusion: The more life change events an individual experiences in a given period of time, the more likely he or she is to become physically ill. Our own bodily data are an important source of awareness regarding our stress levels.

The third area of extensive research on stress and disease is the work done on *heart disease and stress*. Because heart disease (including heart attacks and strokes) has been a serious medical problem and a cause of death for Americans, this is of particular concern to all of us. And I do mean

SOCIAL READJUSTMENT RATING SCALE

HOW TO USE: Add up value of Life Crisis Units for Life Events experienced in two-year period.

  0 to 150—No significant problems

150 to 199—Mild life crisis (33 percent chance of illness)

200 to 299—Moderate life crisis (50 percent chance of illness)

300 or over—Major life crisis (80 percent chance of illness)

RANK	LIFE EVENT	LIFE CRISIS UNITS
1	Death of spouse	100
2	Divorce	73
3	Marital separation	65
4	Jail term	63
5	Death of close family member	63
6	Personal injury or illness	53
7	Marriage	50
8	Fired at work	47
9	Marital reconciliation	45
10	Retirement	45
11	Change in health of family member	44
12	Pregnancy	40
13	Sex difficulties	39
14	Gain of new family member	39
15	Business readjustment	39
16	Change in financial state	38
17	Death of close friend	37
18	Change in different line of work	36
19	Change in number of arguments with spouse	35
20	Mortgage over $10,000	31
21	Foreclosure of mortgage or loan	30
22	Change of responsibilities at work	29
23	Son or daughter leaving home	29
24	Trouble with in-laws	29
25	Outstanding personal achievement	28

SOCIAL READJUSTMENT RATING SCALE
(Continued)

RANK	LIFE EVENT	LIFE CRISIS UNITS
26	Wife begins or stops work	26
27	Begin or end school	26
28	Change in living conditions	25
29	Revision of personal habits	24
30	Trouble with boss	23
31	Change in work hours or conditions	20
32	Change in residence	20
33	Change in school	20
34	Change in recreation	19
35	Change in church activities	19
36	Change in social activities	18
37	Mortgage or loan less than $10,000	17
38	Change in sleeping habits	16
39	Change in number of family get-togethers	15
40	Change in eating habits	15
41	Vacation	13
42	Christmas	12
43	Minor violations of the law	11

The Rahe and Holmes Life Changes Scale. Source: *Journal of Psychosomatic Research*. Vol. 11, 1967. pp. 213–18.

Figure 1–1

all of us. Coronary heart disease is no longer a man's disease or an older man's disease. Younger persons and women have been increasingly susceptible.

The tie-ins between stress and heart disease are numerous. Research studies indicate several interesting possibilities that may well affect many readers. Numerous studies both here and abroad point to the factor of upward mobility as causing significant increases in heart diseases. The stresses of moving out of the socioeconomic position of our childhood and moving up in the world increase the likelihood of coronary heart disease. Other studies suggest related causes. Individuals who frequently change jobs and residences also are more susceptible, as are individuals who lived in or moved to urban industrialized areas (Syme, 1970).

A whole set of different studies with a related result are those done on the coronary-prone (or Type A) personality. Certain personality qualities (usually associated with upward economic mobility) lead to an increased likelihood of heart attacks. These coronary-prone traits include excessive competitiveness and ambition, hostility, impatience, haste, restlessness, difficulties in meeting time restraints, and explosiveness of speech (Rowland & Sokol, 1978).

Is this starting to get close to home? Those of us who recognize our own Type A traits can readily recognize how much our daily stress is aggravated by our impatience, our competitiveness, our haste, and our difficulties in dealing with time. The research here is clear. Those of us possessing these traits are more susceptible to coronary heart disease.

The last point that illustrates dramatically the effect of stress/emotion on our bodies has to do with *muscle tension*. Whenever experiencing emotion/stress, our bodies prepare automatically for some kind of large muscle activity (see Chapter 7 for details). This is the familiar fight/flight reaction. Muscles prepare to move, to contract, to engage in motion. When we do not engage in motion/activity (and typically we do not), the muscles remain tight—we are up tight.

Walt, described in the beginning of this chapter, ended his work day with a "pain in the neck." Often the stresses that develop throughout the day actually seem to accumulate and reside in the muscles. For this reason, a number of the well-respected and traditional methods of stress reduction have focused on relieving muscle tension (see Chapters 7 and 12). Although the physiological details are still not completely understood, one theory (Brown, 1977) emphasizes that muscle fibers, after remaining tense for a period of time, lose their adaptability. Whatever the physiological explanation, the effects on our muscles (whether it is lower back pain, the flare-up of an old football injury, or a headache) are significant. This muscle effect illustrates once again the oneness of body and mind and directs our attention to another way our body reveals to us the condition of our emotional state.

The evidence is substantial. Stress can build up and accumulate in our bodies. And physical symptoms in our bodies are often the first indicators for us of how much stress we are experiencing. Just like the flashing red lights in our cars, our bodies send us warning signals that something is wrong. Our headaches, neckaches, indigestion, and other physical flare-ups are often the first indicators of our rising stress. All of us have our own individual and recurrent body warnings of too much stress. Walt's stress warning was his ache in the neck and shoulders. Yours might be lower back pain, a skin rash, some digestive problem, more frequent colds, and the like.

Take a moment now and make a mental note to yourself to listen more carefully to your body's warning signals. Or perhaps you would find it useful to use the Recall Reminder at the end of this chapter and to write a note to yourself.*

---

* Refer to the "Special Note to Reader" on page xii for an explanation of the Recall Reminders.

RECALL REMINDER

1

OUR ACHING
BODIES

1. Where does stress come out in your body? List the places.

_____   _____

_____   _____

2. Perhaps you'd like to apply the Life Changes Scale to yourself. Circle the *Life Crisis Units* you experienced in the past two years. Add them up. What are your chances of illness?

3. Are you concerned about heart disease? Check the following coronary-prone traits that apply to yourself.

___ Competitive-　　 ___ Restlessness 　　___ Interrupting
     ness 　　　　　　　　　　　　　　　　　　　 others

　　　　　　　　　 ___ Difficulites
___ Ambition 　　　　 with time 　　　 ___ Fast upward
　　　　　　　　　　 restraints 　　　　　 mobility

___ Hostility

___ Impatience

___ Explosiveness in speech

___ Haste

___ Frequent job and geographic changes

2

UNREASONABLE BEHAVIORS

Eleanor was talking about a recent day at work:

> "It had been a rotten day. I hadn't slept well and wasn't feeling my best. When I got to work, I was faced with a pile of letters to type. I started on them, but I made mistake after mistake, became more and more tense. I kept at it doggedly, determined to get through that pile. When my supervisor suggested that I take a break, I blew up and told her I just wanted to finish the darn letters. I realized, though, after having lunch and relaxing a little, that she had been right. I did a much better job after lunch than I had all morning. I don't know why I didn't realize this morning that it would have been more sensible to take a break or work on something other than those letters!"

The reason Eleanor didn't think of alternatives when under stress is what this chapter is all about. The fact is: We just don't think when our emotions are high. Just as we don't feel well or function at our best when we have a physical temperature, our brains don't work well when we have an *emotional* temperature (see Figure 2–1). We don't see options or alternatives. We get caught up in the moment—in our emotions, any emotions. And as our emotional temperatures rise, our rational, reasoning, thinking abilities break down, elude us, or simply disappear.

It may be difficult and even humiliating to face the fact that there are times when we act irrational and unreasonable. I have felt this way. I used to think that as an adult (a psychologist no less!) I should be able to cope with my emotions, to act reasonable all the time. It has been painful to face the fact that I'm not always reasonable, sensible, and pleasant to be with. In situations where my stress level climbs quickly to higher levels, I behave in far from admirable ways. I often talk too much, say the wrong things, hurt

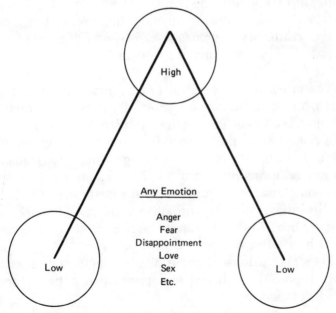

Emotional Temperature—Low to High Intensity
Figure 2–1

other people, or act plain stupid. I disapprove of these behaviors in myself. I've felt ashamed of being unreasonable
and irrational.

This lowering of intellectual ability and functioning is
true of all of us (not just psychologists!). This is not affected
by our education, background, or age. *All human beings at
times act irrational, unreasonable, unreasoning.* The research in this area is aptly summarized in a classic textbook
in this field (Cofer & Appley, 1964).

> . . . But as stress arousal continues, deteriorative
> effects are noticeable in all aspects of perform-
> ance, of judgement, and of relations with others
> and with oneself. Tendencies toward rigidity of
> response, inflexibility, inability to profit from
> experience and to use new information, inability
> to shift when shifting is necessary or to persevere
> when required, suspiciousness, increase in hostil-
> ity, irritability, increase in errors, and decrease in
> speed of performance all appear.

The effect of our emotions and stress on our thinking
and reasoning abilities is an especially important consideration in a book that emphasizes job stress. It is important
here because our intellectual functioning directly affects
our job performance and our work productivity. It also affects our relationships with all the persons we contact at
work—our boss or subordinates, our customers or clients,
our colleagues, patients, students, or others we work with.
These are the people we want to be reasonable and cooperative with, to offer our best to.

Let's take a look at some of the specific changes that
people report in their job and performance behaviors as
stress levels mount.

They behave less sensibly than usual.
They didn't see alternatives or options.

They didn't think of "obvious" possibilities.

They acted unwisely and did not use judgment or experience.

Their point of view was narrowed or highly restricted (they had "tunnel vision").

They had no perspective on the situation.

They were not productive or successful.

Their work was of a poorer quality.

There was wasted activity, spinning of wheels.

They wasted precious time on fruitless self-accusations or dissatisfied feelings.

They really "knew better," but they behaved poorly anyway.

They were not as creative; they didn't come up with the best solution to job tasks and problems.

They were not aware of the consequences of their behaviors.

They acted downright irrational and unreasonable.

They did things they were later ashamed of.

They made more mistakes of all kinds.

They could not "listen" to the other person.

Because all our emotions can cause this lowered intellectual functioning, let's take a look at several different emotions and see their effect (see Figures 2–1 and 2–2). We'll look first at anger. When we are angry (or feel dissatisfied, irritable, or resentful), our emotion is all we are aware of. The more intense our resentment or dissatisfaction, the more unreasonable and insensitive we are. The more irritable and dissatisfied we are, the less clearly we can think. At the beginning of this chapter, Eleanor's irritability and dissatisfaction affected her thinking and her reasonableness. After our anger subsides, when our emotional temperature is lowered, we say to ourselves, "Why didn't I think of saying that or doing that?" We didn't think of it because while our emotions are up toward the peak, we are *incapable of thinking* (see Figure 2–2 again).

Let's move on and consider another emotion—fear—

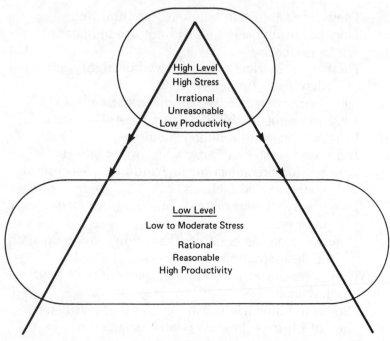

Two Levels of Emotional Temperature
Figure 2–2

and how it affects our rational self. Whether we experience fear of losing our job or a more physical fear for our personal safety, fear typically induces an inability to see options and fosters restricted thinking. In law enforcement, fire protection, the military, and other job situations where individuals can experience intense fear (for their safety and for their very lives), this lack of thinking ability is clearly recognized. Individuals in these fields receive long and careful training so they know how to respond automatically (instinctively), without thinking. They have to respond without thinking because no one thinks while experiencing fear (or any other emotion). After our emotional temperature is lowered (often as a result of behaving as we were trained to do), then we are able to think again (see Figure 2–2).

How about other feelings, such as sexual feelings?

Does any reader recall feeling very rational, sensible, or aware of consequences as he or she feels more and more sexy? Remember the old adage, "Love is blind?" During intense love feelings, we are not especially rational or sensible.

Even while experiencing grief or joy, we are not particularly sensitive to others or aware of the consequences of our behavior. The higher these emotions are towards the peak, the more intensely they are felt, the less our judgment and rationality are available to us.

Take any other emotion—disappointment, hurt, envy, dissatisfaction, or some other. As your emotional temperature rises, recognize how your judgment, intellect, reasonableness, and productivity are lowered. This, as we have pointed out, is true of all of us and is a highly useful indicator of our stress level.

Consider your own work situation. Are you unable to see alternatives for yourself in a stressful situation? This means that your stress/emotion level has risen too high. Are you really unable to listen to what your boss (or a customer, client, or subordinate) is saying, to what his point of view is, to where he is coming from? Do you make more mistakes? Again, your emotional/stress level must be up at the peak (see Figure 2–2). Do you have a client or a customer you just can't understand or don't know where he or she is coming from? Or do you find it impossible to deal with someone you know; do you find that you don't know how to handle him or her? He or she really gets to you. Again, your brain doesn't work when that particular person shoots your emotional temperature up. All these situations have one common symptom: Your brains—that is, your normal intellectual functioning—is lowered or lost.

Make a mental note to remind you of which of these higher stress situations lower your own intellectual functioning (also refer to the examples on pages 18–19). Or use the following Recall Reminder to make notes to yourself.

How do you regain your efficiency and intellectual

functioning? The implication of Figure 2–2 is basic to all the techniques of this book. When you sense that stress (emotion) is rising to those unreasonable and unreasoning higher levels, *take steps to lower your emotional temperature!* And that's what most of this book is all about—increasing your awareness of when stress is mounting and offering you techniques for coping with it.

RECALL REMINDER

UNREASONABLE
BEHAVIORS

Make some notes for yourself on those unreasonable, irrational, nonproductive behaviors you want to avoid. Refer to the list on pages 18–19 and note your own examples.

3
ANGER SITUATIONS

Ted's fed up. It happened again. They made a decision regarding his department without consulting him. No one asked for his opinion or his point of view. And it's a decision that really affects his work, his effectiveness, and his morale. Ted's angry. Right now, he hates his job and would like to quit.

Joan's mad. The boss blamed her again. She feels that the criticism is unfair. She says, "I've been chastised when I'm not even responsible." She's angry at her boss and really dissatisfied with her job.

George is upset. He just finished a job he was working on, and he really blew it. "How could I be so dumb?" He's angry at himself. Whenever he does something wrong, that's the way he feels, and it's not very pleasant.

Rod's also dissatisfied. It was one of those deadlines again. The report had to be in precisely on time. It was a rush job, and he really had to push to meet the deadline. Then Rod discovered that it was sent by "pony express." No one had even looked at it yet. Rod's really teed off.

These are typical job situations where our stress increases as we experience negative, dissatisfied emotions. That general type of emotion will be called *Anger/Dissatisfaction*.

Different individuals, when they think about their own Anger/Dissatisfaction situations, use different words to describe their emotional states. Think about Anger/Dissatisfaction in your own life. What words would you use to describe your negative emotions? People report the following:

Irritated
Annoyed
Being fed up
Frustrated
Dissatisfied
Furious
Enraged
Teed off
Resentful
Being Mad
Angry

I will use the general term *anger/stress* to include our total reactions to any of the above emotional terms.

To help you look at your own anger/stress and to apply the technique in this and the following chapters, think of several situations where you are angry/dissatisfied (remember, any of the above terms may apply).* You can think of your own situations very simply by using the following sentence:

I get angry when_____ does_____.
               (so and so)   (such and such)

---

* Once when I asked a group to do this in a seminar, a man said, "I never get angry." I asked him to think a moment and to consider what term he would use to describe his own situations. After a moment he answered, "I just get mildly p___-off." Use whatever term fits best for you.

So and so, of course, can be any person: your boss, co-worker, spouse, or child—or anyone else, including yourself. Under *such and such*, you fill in what that person did that resulted in your feeling anger/dissatisfaction. Use the Recall Reminder form at the end of this chapter.

When individuals think about their own anger situations at work, here are some of the examples that arouse anger/stress for them. See if you can identify with any of these. I get angry in a work situation when:

> They ask for input from us, and we discover they've already made up their minds.
> I try to finish a job and repeatedly get interrupted.
> I look for answers from my boss and don't get them.
> They change the rules in the middle of the ball game and forget to tell us.
> My supervisor requires me to do something I don't believe in or think is wrong.
> I try to please people and do what they want, and they don't appreciate it.
> I sit in a meeting with highly paid individuals, and everyone avoids the purpose of the meeting.
> Someone assumes that I don't know what I am doing or doesn't give me credit for what I know.
> I have no control over delays.
> They put the pressure on or lay on heavy deadlines.

Managers and supervisors report getting angry when:

> I hear a subordinate being rude to a customer (taxpayer, parent, child, etc.).
> I give instructions, and the individual doesn't pay attention or take notes and then later asks questions I've already answered.
> The rules (code, law, etc.) say no, but people want those rules bent for their own self-interest.
> I repeatedly try to get a subordinate to change his or

her behavior or performance, and he or she doesn't change.

I need information and can't reach a subordinate.

Subordinates don't show job dedication or are apathetic.

A subordinate doesn't follow through, show initiative, or act responsible.

Some typical family situations arouse anger/stress. I get angry when:

My child promises he or she will do something and he or she doesn't do it.

My spouse tells me what's wrong with me.

You teach your kid to be considerate, polite, and cooperative, and other people teach their kids to be rude.

My wife (girlfriend) tells me about her old boyfriends.

My child disobeys, won't clean his room, and so on.

My husband gets angry at me.

My son does a dumb thing.

My kid argues with me.

My daughter doesn't do her homework.

Other situations arouse our anger/stress, too. I get angry when:

I'm waiting in a long line, and someone sneaks in ahead of me.

People complain incessantly.

The neighbors make a lot of noise.

The clerks are discourteous or not interested in serving me.

My cat defecates on the rug.

The Padres lose a game.

I come home tired, and the kids next door have their bicycles dumped in my driveway.

I have to wait in lines at the bank, post office, cashier, and so on.

Situations that arouse anger/stress while driving in a car include the following. I get angry when:

That idiot on the freeway passes me, going like crazy.
A car suddenly cuts in front of me.
Someone drives slow in the fast lane.
On a two-lane road, I come up to someone who is driving very slowly.
Drivers weave back and forth around me.

Anger/stress can be aroused when we get angry at ourselves. I get angry when:

I can't say "no" to people.
I feel I've been taken advantage of.
I back away and feel I should have been more aggressive.
I can't help someone I want to help.
I haven't the guts to deal with a person or situation.
I make a mistake or do a poor job.
I don't handle a situation or problem the way I feel I should.
I don't live up to my own high expectations.

As you think about your own job/family stresses, you can probably identify with one or more of the above. You may also recall situations different from the ones listed. Most individuals recognize a number of these situations in their lives.

Whatever the number of your own anger/stress situations (and sometimes we can fill up a whole page with them) what is crucial is the nature of the methods you use to deal with them.

There are three methods of handling anger that typically increase our stress levels and sometimes do so considerably. These three methods are as follows:

1. We put other people down.
2. We transfer anger from job to family.
3. We accumulate anger in our bodies.

We have already discussed accumulating anger in Chapter 1. In this chapter, we will consider in detail putting people down, and in Chapter 4, we will talk about transferring anger to family situations.

When we are experiencing anger (irritation, annoyance, dissatisfaction, resentment, etc.), a typical way we have of dealing with that anger is to put someone down. Sometimes we put them down verbally; sometimes we put them down with our body language, facial expression, or manner. Sometimes our put-downs are expressed; at other times, we say them only to ourselves, keeping them inside our own thoughts. There are lots of different techniques for putting people down. Individuals report the following variety. Get out your own list and compare it to the following:

Label them "dumb," "inconsiderate," "lazy," "deadhead," and a host of other name-calling terms.

Reject them—give them the cold shoulder, exclude them, treat them with silence, or ignore them.

Attack their competence, their bodies, their mental capacities, their relatives, and so on.

So-called humor—making fun of people or telling jokes at their expense.

Blame them.

Ridicule them.

Criticize them—"constructively" or otherwise.

Tear down their esteem and their confidence—either directly or by gossiping about them to others.

Use sarcasm—say, "Good afternoon" to a subordinate as he comes in late.

Act sullen or hurt; mope or sulk (I'm very good at
    doing this).
Hurt them in any other way, verbally or nonverbally.

Perhaps your list includes some other techniques not mentioned above. We all seem to have put-down methods, developed over the years, that we use—usually with considerable skill. At times, we may use them frequently; at other
times, but rarely. And remember, too, that these put-downs
can be expressed either outwardly and directly to a person
or remain verbally unexpressed. If not expressed verbally,
they will remain in our minds as a seemingly endless circle
of blaming and attacking feelings. They continue to color
our attitude toward the person we dislike. They may even
be expressed nonverbally without our being aware of it.

Who do we put down? At work, there are a variety of
possibilities. The following are the more obvious:

Subordinates (people we supervise or manage).
Persons in jobs below us on the ladder (that poor guy at
    the bottom!).
Any person in a group whom we don't like (those
    dumb so and so's).
Persons in any other work group, particularly in a com-
    peting group.
Persons in a racial or nationality group generally
    looked down upon.
Individuals used as scapegoats (poor Charlie).
The boss (but not to his face).
Ourselves (the real culprit?).
Customers, clients, taxpayers, students, parents, and
    so on.

Check out your put-down list and see who seems to get it
the most.

I've said that put-downs are one of three methods that
severely increase our stress levels. Why would put-downs
increase our level of stress, resulting therefore in adverse

feelings, behaviors, or body reactions? (Refer, if necessary, to Chapter 1.) Let's take a look at the reasons for this.

When we put someone down, however enjoyable that may momentarily seem to us, we generally create new problems for ourselves. The kinds of stresses created are as follows:

1. We feel guilty or wrong about putting someone down.
2. We arouse a negative reaction in the person we put down and face the short- or long-term consequences of doing that.
3. We don't solve the anger/stress situation that upset us in the first place.
4. The expressed anger may feed itself and raise us to even higher emotional levels.

Let's look at these in detail. As we do this, consider your own anger/stress situations. Is some of your stress caused by your using put-downs?

First of all, most people report that they feel guilty about putting someone down. Personally, whenever I put someone down, I feel it's wrong. Using put-downs often leaves us dissatisfied with ourselves; we may even feel more anger/stress. Sometimes we may feel a need to make amends. We feel strained, unsettled, and uncomfortable.

Most importantly, we inevitably arouse a negative reaction in the person we have put down. This negative reaction can also spread to anyone present who witnessed the put-down or to others who just hear of it. This reaction can have consequences for us, either directly or indirectly.

If the reaction is direct, the other person puts us down in turn, and the typical result is an argument or battle. Arguments are typically nonproductive and highly stress-arousing. While in the middle of an argument, we are not particularly rational, reasonable, or sensible.

If the other person does not argue with you, you can be

sure that his or her negative reaction will be expressed indirectly. In a work situation, there are endless opportunities for indirect expression. Let's take a look at some of them. The individual you put down may:

Feel unhelpful toward you in the future.
Feel less spontaneous willingness to cooperate with you in a task.
Generally slow down in work productivity.
Feel less team cohesiveness or have poor morale.
Sabotage your efforts, office work, and so on.
Gossip behind your back.
Harbor hidden agendas that interfere in meetings, in making decisions, and in getting things done.

Let's take a look at some of these indirect anger consequences. Indirect methods are often hidden from obvious view, but they are very real and very powerful. Let's consider for a moment how we react if someone puts us down. Typically, we just don't feel very favorable toward that person. Generally, we don't enjoy working with him or her; we don't feel a part of a work team if he or she is a member of it. If it's a boss who puts us down, we don't go the extra mile in helping him or her or go out of our way to do a superb job. We often find it difficult to communicate with the person, possibly for some time afterward. Sometimes we just don't seem to understand what he or she is saying. Or we experience emotional rejection in ourselves whenever he or she talks, or asks for a request, or offers a suggestion. These negative effects of put-downs lower our work efficiency considerably. With these kinds of feelings and reactions, it can take a lot longer to get things done.

Just remember that when you use a put-down at work, you may be arousing just such reactions and agendas in coworkers and subordinates. Hidden agendas are also sneaky little influences that cause a waste of time. Did you ever wonder why some little, unimportant decision can arouse such long disagreement and discussion? There are obviously feelings under the surface that have nothing to do with the situation at hand. These feelings can be left over from past hurts, from unresolved problems, and from times when individuals have been put down and have kept that feeling inside. Much time can be wasted at meetings and at group problem-solving sessions. Getting input on a problem from a group can arouse these hidden agendas and considerably hinder the decision-making process. All this results from previous put-downs that are still alive underneath. These reactions create stress for all concerned, especially for the individuals who have responsibility for getting things done.

The third way that put-downs increase our stress is by not solving anything. Putting someone down at work when we are angry and dissatisfied does not solve the problem that bothered us. Take a look again at your anger/stress situations. Very few of them are changed or solved to your satisfaction by putting someone down. We still have the stresses of that unresolved anger and dissatisfaction. On top of that, we have piled up further stresses for ourselves by arousing negative reactions in others and in ourselves. We have made a bad situation worse.

Some people report that getting angry in itself creates stress for them. Anger is an emotion that many of us have been taught to disapprove of. It's just not nice; it's uncomfortable. I can still feel some fear in the presence of someone's anger. Just getting angry enough to put someone down makes us recognize how uncontrolled we have become or how irrationally we are behaving. For some of us, perhaps for those of us who have a Mediterranean heritage, anger can feed more anger. Once we get started expressing our anger, some of us find it easy to push up our emotional temperature, running ourselves right off the scale. The result is a highly stressed individual—ourselves!

Does anger cause you heightened discomfort, fear, or disapproval? Or does getting angry spiral upward and feed fuel to your emotional fires? Either way, your stress level is higher. And a higher stress level produces all the inevitable reactions to your body, your rationalness, your productivity.

In summary, then, let's begin to take a look at the inevitable job-related anger and dissatisfaction. Consider your own work anger/dissatisfaction in its varied forms. Are you dealing with any of it by putting other people down, either verbally or in your fantasies? Consider the complications and the loss of spending your time and energies doing just that. Consider the stresses and problems created and the unresolved problems still waiting to be dealt with. Make a note to yourself on the Recall Reminder on page 34 of the people you want to stop putting down in order to reduce your own stress. And then move on to the next chapters, where we will consider other ways we have of coping with the anger/dissatisfaction that creates stress for ourselves.

RECALL REMINDER

3

ANGER SITUATIONS

I'd like to remember certain anger situations that really bother me.

1. I get angry (irritated, frustrated) when

_____ does _____ .

(so and so)   (such and such)

2. "I also get angry _____ ."

_____ ."

3. "I also get angry _____ ."

Right now (when I am reasonable), I would like to recall that I want to stop putting down:

_____ (List the people)

_____

_____

4
DUMPING STRESS ON OUR FAMILIES

I'm sure you probably remember the old story about transferring anger and stress: The husband gets bawled out by his boss; he says nothing to the boss but takes it home, snaps at his wife, and complains about the lousy meal she cooked. She's possibly sensitive to what happened at work and doesn't bitch back; but instead, she yells at her twelve-year-old daughter. The daughter, in turn, hits her nine-year-old brother, who eventually kicks the dog. I suppose if you believe in justice, the dog takes off down the street, finds the boss's house, and bites him.

With or without the final act of retribution, most of us can recognize ourselves in this kind of situation. We wouldn't be honest with ourselves if we didn't admit that there are times when we dump job stress on our families. We take home the stress that develops inevitably in work situations and then proceed to dump it on our spouses or children, on close friends or other intimates, or on our relatives or parents. When we do this, we find that we use any of a variety of put-downs listed in previous Chapter 3. In this case, however, we put down someone we love, someone we care for, and someone who loves us.

As strange as this might seem at first thought; it is hardly so. It is not at all strange in the sense of being rare. It is frequently done. Possibly, though I have no statistical evidence to support this, transferring stress to one's family may be the most frequently used method for the handling of job-aroused anger/stress. It is also not strange in that there are explanations. As people think about the reasons why they choose loved ones to get angry at, the explanation offered is usually one or more of the following:

> They are available.
> They are safe to dump on (that is, relatively safe).
> They won't hurt you (not in the way a boss or coworker can).
> Their personalities might be receptive to this.
> They will still love us (this we will discuss later in the chapter).
> They won't reject us.
> They might understand us (if their emotional temperature is not too high).

It's really quite easy to dump on our families. Home is the place to let your hair down, to be yourself, it's the place to express what you can't (or won't) express elsewhere. Because people in our families love us, they "should" discount our anger and recognize it for what it is. It may be easy, too, to dump on families because we are merely modeling what we experienced in our own childhood: our own parents taking out their anger/dissatisfaction on each other or taking it out on their children.

It's easy, too, because of cultural support: Television, comics, and other social reinforcers do it. We may even at times consider it humorous (as long as it's not happening to us).

And yet dumping on our families is not where it's at. It, too, tends to increase rather than decrease our stress levels.

The consequences, now or later, can be disastrous. The eventual effects on our bodies, rationalness, and productivity can be considerable.

The reasons why transferring anger to our families carries with it the likelihood of further stress are as follows:

1. We feel wrong about it, or we feel guilty (just like any other put-down).
2. We feel even more uncomfortable with it because we know our families are not the cause of the problem.
3. Letting loose on spouses and children doesn't solve the job/anger/stress situation.
4. It escalates or expands our stress areas from our jobs to our marriages, our families, and our children.
5. Sooner or later (sometimes sooner than you think) it cuts off sources of support, affection, and love (all of which we need in order to cope with stress).
6. It can, unfortunately, too easily lead to two very severe problems: divorce and child abuse.

Many individuals recognize the severity of the strain on their families as job pressures increase or as job anxiety mounts. How much the marriage can take, the family can take, or our children can take can be assessed by our spouses and children self-monitoring their own feelings, behavior, and body reactions. If we dump sufficiently on our families to lessen their love feelings for us and to cause them to behave in an angry, negative fashion toward us, we lose a great deal. And, of course, soemtimes the loss is permanent: The marriage dissolves, or our children turn away from us.

Take a few moments to look at your own anger/stress situations (see Chapter 3). How do you handle that job anger/dissatisfaction? How much of it affects the love and stability of your close relationships and your marriage and family ties? Is there a danger that you are cutting off affection, caring, and love from your spouse or partner or children?

If this causes you some concern, you will want to seek other methods for handling anger/stress. Make some notes to yourself on the Recall Reminder sheet to remind you that you want to stop taking out your anger/dissatisfaction on your family. In particular, you will want to look for stress-reduction methods in this book that mediate between the work/job part of your day and the family/loved one part of your day. You will want to break that pattern of transferring. Read on.

RECALL REMINDER

4
DUMPING STRESS ON OUR FAMILIES

I'd like to stop taking my anger/stress home and sometimes dumping it on the following family members:

_____

_____

_____

_____

5

IS MY STRESS LEVEL TOO HIGH?

George's week hadn't been going too well. Last night he'd been up late. He and his wife had had another talk about their fifteen-year-old son, a talk that had degenerated into a blaming argument. When he awoke, he was weary and unrested. He felt restless, and during breakfast he was clearly irritable and not very pleasant to be around. When he finally got off to work, the traffic was heavy. He impatiently changed lanes a lot and honked his horn several times. Later, when he arrived at work, his desk seemed overflowing with unfinished business. Today was no exception—problems and headaches. Several people, too, were waiting with dissatisfactions and complaints. He wasn't able to listen to them very patiently; he certainly wasn't particularly tolerant of their points of view. Throughout the morning, he found his mind wandering as other people talked to him. He just couldn't focus on several big projects he had planned to tackle. He drank five or six cups of coffee during the morning and stuffed in a dough-nut or two with each cup. When lunch time arrived, he felt a need for a drink and wanted nothing more than to escape—

get away from it all. But he had an early afternoon meeting, so he gulped a quick lunch and went back to his office to get ready for it. All he remembered of the meeting was his indigestion. The rest of the afternoon was quieter but not much better. He snapped at his secretary once or twice and was curt with colleagues. He felt weary, tense, and tight. He again postponed several decisions. He finished one report but wasn't too pleased with it.

When he arrived at home, he wanted nothing more than a drink and a chance to spout off about how hard he worked and how lousy his job was. Later that night, as he looked back calmly on the day, he noted that nothing extraordinary had occurred: There had been no serious crises or any extremely negative experiences. Yet it had been a stressful day; one during which he clearly had not been at his best and had not given his best.

Why did George let his stress accumulate all day without doing something about it? How can we recognize where our stress level is and avoid letting the stress gain control (as George's did)? These are the basic questions for stress management to be explored in this chapter. First, let's consider the issue of why we often are just not aware of how stressed we are.

Sometimes, of course, it *is* obvious. We fall to pieces. We get sick, cop out, drop out, become depressed. If it continues, we may have a breakdown, get divorced, or lose our jobs. In milder forms, we grimly hold on, keeping our noses to the grindstone and patching ourselves together very, very tenuously. We overeat; overconsume sugar; overload on alcohol, caffeine, or tobacco. We use some form of "glue" or "bandaid" that holds us together, barely hiding the serious problems or anxiety underneath. We all know these more obvious states of stress; we've all been there, in one form or another.

Sometimes the obvious state happens suddenly and is over with just as suddenly. We quickly rise to a high level of

stress, often with anger. While up there, we act pretty dumb
or say things we are sorry for later; but we quickly (or fairly
quickly) regain our senses, lower our stress levels, and become more rational and reasonable again.

Often, however, our situation is more like George's. It's
a slow accumulation, not a sudden, spontaneous outburst. It
may be building up for days or even months. It's not so
obvious. George kept going. Yet he was far from his best. He
was not as pleasant to be around. He was not arousing feelings of cooperation and friendliness in people he made contact with all day or all week. Most importantly, he wasn't
performing at his best, his productivity was not that great,
and the quality of his work behavior was lower than he was
capable of. It might seem obvious, from the viewpoint of an
outside observer, that George was acting pretty dumb. To
George, it wasn't obvious.

Why aren't we always aware of what stresses happen to
us so that we can take steps to get out of a poor stress state?
What prevents us from taking control of our situations and
making them better?

There are at least three elements at work in George's
situation, any of which may fit for any of us. Some of these
have been explored in depth in previous chapters.

<u>First,</u> George's stress level rose slowly, not rapidly. He
adapted to his stress each step of the way. Slow changes are
not always obvious to us; they are insidious. They dull our
awareness. We don't know how tall our son has grown in
the last six months until a relative who hasn't seen him
points it out to us. Then we recognize the change. No
one—all day or all week—pointed out the change to
George.

<u>Next,</u> as our stress rises, we have seen (see Chapter 2)
that our intellectual awareness drops. Our brains are not
operating in full swing. Those emotions get in the way. We
tune into the emotion of dissatisfaction, disappointment, or
frustration, *not* into an intellectual awareness of how these

feelings are affecting our performance, our job functioning, and our total behavior. Under high stress, our emotions hold sway.

<u>Finally</u>, when we try to gain awareness, we have lots of good reasons for fooling ourselves (see Chapter 6). We rely on our adapted feelings, our need to defend ourselves (however indefensible!), and our need to bolster our lowered esteem. We try, however desperately, to live up to that cool, calm ideal. We fool ourselves into "feeling" that everything is okay—that it's really not that bad.

These are three danger points. They are clearly to be avoided if we are to manage our stress well. How can we manage to escape George's route and gain a more accurate awareness of our stress levels?

The previous chapters all lead us to the basic tool of this section: *regular monitoring of our stress level.* We must take the time to assess those levels and use that time to collect data regarding our stress levels, seeking out relevant, accurate data.

The entire process is simple and may be summarized in three steps.

> **STEP 1:** Collect as much data as you can on yourself.
> **STEP 2:** Using this data, make a decision as to whether your stress level is too high.
> **STEP 3:** If necessary, take action to lower your stress to more reasonable, productive levels.

Let's take a look at Steps 1 and 2. A good deal of the remainder of this book will deal with the third step, the alternative methods we can use to lower stress.

Step 1: Collect as much data on yourself as you can. Collect the data in three areas:

1. Your total behaviors.

2. Your body reactions.
3. Your feelings.

Let's see how this works by applying Step 1 to two different situations. First of all, let's apply it to a "good" stress situation. This is where our stress level is not high or excessive (see Level I in figure 5–1).

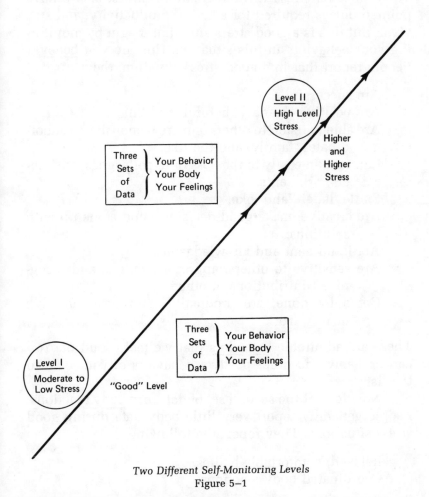

Level II
High Level
Stress

Higher
and
Higher
Stress

Three
Sets
of
Data } Your Behavior
Your Body
Your Feelings

Three
Sets
of
Data } Your Behavior
Your Body
Your Feelings

Level I
Moderate to
Low Stress

"Good" Level

Two Different Self-Monitoring Levels
Figure 5–1

Think of a comfortable stress situation, such as one of the following:

> A challenging, interesting work activity.
> An exciting, satisfying project at work.
> A satisfying, successful sales or some other challenge.
> A pleasurable family or friendly relationship.

There is some stress in this situation. Stress, as we have pointed out, is required for activity, productivity, and survival. But this is a good stress situation. Begin by monitoring your **behaviors** in this situation. How do you **behave**? People report that in a good stress situation, they:

> Are successful.
> Are positive, friendly, helpful, and "nice."
> Are able to listen to others and are responsive to subordinates, family, and the like.
> Can tune in easily to the boss or to colleagues, customers, or clients.
> Smile, laugh, and joke.
> Are creative, make good decisions, and come up with solutions.
> Act intelligent and knowledgable.
> Are sensitive to others, appreciate others, and recognize contributions of others.
> Get a lot done, are productive, and turn out high quality work.

These are admirable **behaviors** that we feel proud of. You can probably add other **positive** behaviors of your own to the list.

Now look at the second set of data, our **body reactions**. People generally report very little body data during good stress situations. They report the following:

> Relaxed, comfortable bodies.
> Coordinated body reactions.

They are not aware of their bodies which operate
 smoothly.
There is an absence of ill health and of aches and pains.

This is probably the good health area where our smoothly
functioning bodies are sending none of those aching, un-
healthy signals we get at other times.

Last, look at the third set of data—your <u>feelings</u>. What
feelings do you have in such a situation? People report the
following <u>feelings</u> in these good situations:

Excitement or exhilaration.
Pleasure or enjoyment.
Relaxation or calmness.
Action or movement.
Confidence or sureness.

You may recognize one or more of these feelings. Or possibly you recall some other feelings that we usually identify
as "positive" feelings. Remember that we have been monitoring a good stress situation. You must be able to recall at
least one good stress situation in order to do this. Some of
you may feel that you have to dig deep into the past to do
this (remember ten years ago—was it on a Thursday?). But
do it.

Next, apply Step 2 at this point. You have already assessed your behavior, your body, and your feelings. The
total picture looks good. The data in all three areas are positive: We have no problems, all systems are "go," and our
stress level is okay.

Now, let's apply Step 1 of self-monitoring to a high
stress level (see Figure 5–1). Here, the situation is different.
Recall George's day, or recall your own "not so good" stress
situation, one you experienced in the last week or two. You

will probably have no trouble recalling at least one such situation. Some examples to stir your memory tapes follow:

> Before a tense conference with the boss or after receiving a criticism.
> During an argument with a spouse, friend, colleague, child, or subordinate.
> While facing deadlines, pressures, or responsibilities.
> In a frustrating or boring staff meeting.
> Hearing some negative gossip about yourself.
> After "blowing it."
> Serious family sickness or loss.

Let's look at the first set of data—our <u>behaviors</u>. What were George's behaviors like all day?

> He engaged in some wasted motion and activity.
> He was irritable; he even put people down.
> He was not pleasant to be around.
> He was not aware of alternatives or of other ways to behave.
> He let little things get to him.
> He was impatient.
> He reached for the caffeine and the alcohol.
> His work quality was down.
> He avoided coping with decisions.

Do you recognize any of these? Or perhaps some of the other behaviors listed in Chapter 2 on pages 18–19 fit your own high stress situations. Take another look at that list.

Telling it like it is, we aren't behaving that well. Far from our creditable side, not our most admirable behaviors. Not the way we want to behave toward others, not the way we want to perform in our work.

Let's now move to the second set of data. What happens to our <u>bodies</u> as stress increases? George experienced indigestion, tenseness, and muscle tension. People report a variety of other body reactions, such as the following:

Various aches and pains, such as headaches and neck-aches (pain in the neck!).

Backache or lower back pain (pain in the a——!).

Varied stomach and digestive disorders and upsets or ulcers.

Overeating; high sugar consumption; more alcohol, tobacco, or caffeine.

Sleep disturbances.

Skin rashes, itches, and assorted skin irritations.

Breathing irregularities or asthma.

Tense, tight muscles.

Tics or dandruff.

Heart disease.

Just about any other illness (recall Chapter 1).

What happens to your body? Most people report one particular body symptom that most frequently expresses their stress. That symptom can be viewed as a message from your body telling you what's happening to your stress level. Add it to your other data.

Now, let's check out the high stress situation by looking at the third set of data—our feelings. We aren't going to rely solely on this data (see Chapter 6). During his day, George felt briefly angry; he felt much dissatisfaction. At various times, he felt restless, unsure, and even concerned about his job adequacy and competence. He also felt overwhelmed, rushed, and tense. He may have felt other feelings, perhaps less clearly. People report under high stress a host of negative, unpleasant feelings, such as the following:

Anxious, timid, or fearful.

Angry, resentful, dissatisfied, or bitter.

Confused, overwhelmed, or swamped.

Helpless or powerless.
Fear of inadequacy or failure.
Tense or tight.
Depressed, weary, or fed up.
Paranoid*

Perhaps you have had other feelings. The above list gives you some idea of the range of feelings that people can experience. Later on, Chapter 8 will include an even broader list.

You have collected data in all three areas. Now you are ready to go on to Steps 2 and 3 of Stress Management. In Step 2, you must make a decision about your stress level, and decide whether you want to change. Then, if necessary, move to Step 3 and take action to lower your stress level.

These are some of the questions people ask themselves in making the decision in Step 2:

> Am I satisfied, comfortable with my <u>behaviors,</u> my <u>body</u>, and my <u>feelings</u>?
> Do I want to live with the consequences of these reactions—the cost to me in relationships, health, and all the trade-offs?
> How *long* can I keep going with these behaviors, body reactions, and feelings?

Or perhaps you will ask even more deeply felt questions, such as the following:

> If I continue to behave in this way, what will happen to my crucial relationships with my spouse, my children, and my boss?
> Is this what I want out of life, how I want to spend my life?

---

* A school administrator offered this feeling in a large meeting on stress. He said he felt paranoid during high stress situations. I answered, "If you're a school administrator, you aren't paranoid. They really are out to get you!" How about your profession? I'm sure many readers can identify!

Are these reactions consistent with what I want to be as a human being?

The judgment, of course, is yours. Where on Figure 5–1 do you place your stress level? Should you take steps to change your stress level? The decision is all yours.

This decision-making process was dramatically illustrated several years ago during one of my stress management seminars. An older man who had had a recent heart attack brought a younger thirty-nine-year-old man to a session of the seminar. The two men had recently met as patients in the intensive care unit of the hospital where both were recovering from heart attacks. The older man wanted to live longer and had made the decision that it would be necessary to change his high stress behavior (Step 2). He wanted to help his thirty-nine-year-old hospital acquaintance avoid another heart attack. The younger man sat through the entire session without a word. Afterwards he came up to me and said, "All those behaviors are mine. I'm a classic case. But if I change, I'm afraid I'll lose all I've worked so long and so hard for." He left and never returned. He had made his decision. Make yours.

RECALL REMINDER

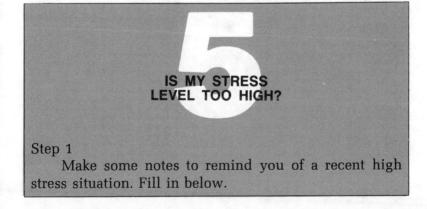

IS MY STRESS LEVEL TOO HIGH?

Step 1
　　Make some notes to remind you of a recent high stress situation. Fill in below.

1. Your behaviors:

2. Your body:

3. Your feelings:

Step 2

  Make the judgment: Was your stress level too high?

DON'T TRUST
YOUR FEELINGS

There is a potential difficulty to be aware of as we answer the basic question of Chapter 5, "Is my stress level too high?" This difficulty stems from a natural human tendency to ask ourselves, "How do I feel?" and to use the answer as a means of determining how high our stress levels are. There is a danger in relying too heavily on our feelings as a source of data about stress. This danger stems from the fact that our feelings can hide from us an accurate view of our stress load and its total effect on us.

Let's take a look at several examples. Mike has just arrived home from work. He slams the door, struts into the house, and disappears into the living room. He utters a few sighs and groans as he plops into his chair. He retreats behind his newspaper, but suddenly he snaps out and reprimands the kids. He pulls back again into his sullen state. He's not talking at all about his day at work. His wife gently asks, "What's bothering you, dear?" He snaps back, "I'm fine." He turns on the TV, and that's that. Everyone in his family knows Mike is upset, but he's not facing it himself.

Right now, Mike is not ready to admit to himself what's

bothering him. He's not ready to face what's happening in his job or how he is behaving toward his wife and kids. He's trying to act like he is in control, like he's still on top of things. If he asks himself how he *feels*, he doesn't get an accurate view of his stress level. You may find that in many high stress situations, your conscious *feelings* do not accurately tell you your total stress picture.

Here's another example that illustrates how deceptive our feelings can be. You are looking for a home, and the real estate agent shows you one near a jet airport, one that is close to a noisy sports stadium where a high-school band is practicing, or perhaps one next to a busy freeway. The noise bothers you, and you ask the owners how they feel about it. "Does the noise bother you?" The husband answers, "It used to when we first moved here, but you get used to it." The wife says, "I've adjusted to it. I just tune it out and don't hear it anymore." Both the husband and wife have very effectively tuned out their feelings to the noise. But if they are living near a jet airport, let's hope this woman isn't pregnant. One study showed a more than 30% increase in abnormal births for pregnant women who lived in the flight path of Los Angeles International Airport, compared to other pregnant women living in Los Angeles County. Numerous studies on noise and stress have demonstrated clearly that noise almost always has an adverse effect on stress (Jansen, 1971) and that we do not really adapt to it (even though we may consciously feel better about it). Here again, our *feelings* do not really tell us what is happening to our behaviors and to our bodies. Like Mike, people who live in noisy situations cannot rely on what they are feeling to tell them what is really happening to their stress levels.

Here's still another example, an everyday one. Driving a car is so typical an activity today that it is rare to find someone who doesn't drive. And often our driving is through traffic or during rush hours. It involves weaving in and out, stopping and going, accelerating, and hitting the brake. It is tense, busy, and active. We experience close shaves, near accidents, and the like. But if you ask most people how they feel about driving (and I do ask people that question often), the most frequent answers are, "I enjoy it," "It's okay," "I don't mind it," "You adjust to it," "I'm comfortable with it," and the like.

And yet research studies have shown that driving is an extremely stressful situation for most people; in some cases, there are even serious consequences to our cardiovascular and hormonal conditions. Carruthers, and English pathologist, studied both the continuous EKG action of the heart and the stress hormone increase in individuals while they drove cars in traffic. Mostly drivers said that they felt "relaxed and not hurrying." The results were not consistent with their conscious feelings. In overtaking other cars, stress levels mounted. One perfectly fit young woman actually had a heart attack while driving! Persons with any previous heart trouble had "spectacularly abnormal electrical activity on their EKG's" (Carruthers, 1974).

Here again, we cannot trust our conscious awareness. These feelings have adapted and they no longer tell us the whole story of our stress reactions. You have convinced yourself that you are relaxed and comfortable, but what actually is happening to your behavior, your *heart,* and the rest of your body?

Here's another example, a personal one. Years ago I had a particularly stressful public job. I worked long hours, there were many demands, and I was often under public attack. How did I *feel* about it? I was excited and stimulated. As I look back now on the situation, if anyone had asked the people who saw me intimately every day for an accurate picture of how I behaved, the picture would not have been that rosy. The situation in actual fact was so bad that I was divorced within a year! I was trying hard to live up to the cool, calm, executive image. I was faking myself out. My total behaviors were not at all consistent with my feelings.

Since we are quite capable at times of fooling ourselves, how can we guard against this danger? How can we increase the accuracy of our self-monitoring?

The best antidote for putting too much confidence in our immediate feelings is to collect as much data as possible on our behavior and on our bodies. The following are some suggestions for becoming more aware of your total behavior and your body. The basic rule is: *Get more data; don't rely solely on your feelings.*

Your total behaviors: Here is where you can get tremendously helpful input from others. Check out the following possibilities:

1. Gather courage and ask your spouse or partner for an honest picture of how you behaved during your last stress episode. Check it out against the list in Chapter 2, pages 18–19). Remember to do this only *after* you have lowered your own emotional temperature sufficiently so that your brains and thinking are operating at your normal reasonable level (see Figure 2–2). Your lowered emotional temperature will considerably increase the chances that you will respond to this input in a reasonable and rational fashion. Don't ask for input when you are at higher stress levels. The response you get will probably shoot your emotional temperature right off the graph. Often this input on your behavior is best given and received in an atmosphere of caring and love. Choose a good time for both you and your spouse. Don't stack it against yourself.

2. If you have a secretary, gather your courage again and ask for input from your secretary. Ask for data regarding your behavior in previous stress episodes—for example, after returning from a tense committee meeting, from a bad conference with the boss, or from a situation where your performance or adequacy was questioned. Get a dialogue going with your secretary. Your secretary will probably start sharing his or her own stress situations, and you might learn some significant new information about what goes on in your office. This opens up more understanding between

boss and secretary, including better feelings and more cooperative responses in the future. If you don't have a secretary,
ask a friend at work, a colleague, or a coworker. "Tell me,
I'm ready for it: How do I really behave under stress? I want
the data in order to help me understand myself better, to
help me know when to take action to lower my stress level."
Choose a coworker who can be of help, and you will gain
valuable data. Some people report that they are able to ask
for this kind of input from the persons who supervise or
direct them. This can obviously develop into a highly satisfactory boss—subordinate relationship.

3. Remember that the purpose of this input is to *help*
you. Don't get hung up in judgmental statements that are
mixed in with the behavior input. For example, if your
spouse or secretary says, "That was a terrible way to behave," ignore that part of the input and ask, "What, specifically, did I do?" Then you may discover that you rushed
madly about the office or house, that you acted the heavy
with a small child, that you pulled your rank on some subordinate, that you gave someone a suggestion he or she
didn't want, or that you acted irritable and snappish. Again,
ask for this input only when your emotional temperature is
low, and don't let any judgmental part of the input raise
your emotional temperature again. Remember: The purpose
of the input is to help you. Don't say anything that will raise
the other person's emotional temperature. Keep the interaction at a caring, seeking, helping level!

4. Who would *you* like to ask for input? Who could
you have a caring, positive dialogue with about stress?
Make a mental note or use the Recall Reminder on page 57.

Next, also check out your body reactions more carefully. Do the following:

1. Tune into the messages from your body: When do
you eat more, crave sweets more, smoke more, or reach for
the alcohol? These are probably times of heightened stress.

2. Listen to the physical signals: Are you getting more
colds, flu, illnesses, aches, and pains? Is your "bad knee"

flaring up, your headaches, your digestive trouble, your lower back pain, and so on? Are you reaching more for the blood pressure pills, the antacid pills or digestive remedies, the digitalis, and so on? Are you taking more tranquilizers? Sleeping pills?

3. What's the medical input been like the past few years? For how many symptoms does the physician say, "We can't find any physical causes?" Or has your physician asked you directly about your stress level? Has your blood pressure been high or fluctuating? Are you having more "accidents?" Some studies of visits by patients to general practitioners estimate that as many as 85% of those visits involved emotional (stress) factors on the part of the patient (Arieti, 1975).

In summary, the basic lesson here is emphatic: Don't rely on those feelings alone. Feelings can be quite misleading! Don't fool yourself. Unfortunately, it's too easy to do just that. We've all done it.

Take a risk! Ask for input. Get all the data you can. And when you get that input, it's usually a rewarding experience. Give it a try.

RECALL REMINDER

DON'T TRUST YOUR FEELINGS

We've seen that we can't always rely on our feelings because we are all capable of fooling ourselves.

The best way to prevent that from happening is to get data from other people on how we behave. Who could

give you help in identifying your behaviors under stress?
List their names here:

_____

_____

_____

_____

BREAKING
THE PATTERN

7

DON'T TALK—
WALK!

Jack's been fuming all day. It was Bill again. Jack supervises Bill, and at times, it can be a real headache. Bill's a good worker, but often he doesn't respond well to supervision. Today's problem started last week. Jack went over Bill's new project with him, made some telling criticisms of the basic approach, and felt quite justified in the cost and marketing problems involved. Bill, as usual, resisted this, but he finally seemed to accept his supervisor's point of view. It was a real shock to Jack this morning to discover that Bill had gone over his head. He had mentioned his project to Jack's boss; the response, Bill reported, had been enthusiastic. Jack had been bypassed without his knowledge; his decision had been reversed by his own superior. Jack was shocked and angry. He muttered something like "We'll see about that" and took off for his own office. He wasn't sure yet what he wanted to do about it. He started on his in-basket and found it hard to concentrate. He alternated all morning between trying to forget the incident and thinking of how he should handle it. Inside, he was seething. He decided to see his boss and "have it out," but fortunately his boss was out of town. Jack kept most of his dissatisfaction, frustration, disappointment, and anger inside. Not all of it, however. His secretary knew things weren't right. He had trouble concentrating on detailed problems. He was a bit snappy with a customer—more irritable, not quite like his usual self. By closing time, Jack had a mild headache and felt tense. He wanted nothing more than to get home and have a drink.

How could Jack have handled his stress differently? How could he have avoided stewing all day with his anger, having it affect his work and his contacts with people? This chapter will discuss in considerable detail a technique called Large Muscle Activity (hereafter called LMA). This is a technique Jack could have used right at work to return himself to his normal and reasonable stress level.

LMA is an especially useful technique. Its power lies in its directness in lowering anger/stress and its speed in doing so. This technique is also valuable because it probably works for more people than any other single technique. There is no magical recipe for anger/stress. No drug, pill, or vitamin can solve our anger/stress situations. Nor is there a single technique that seems to work for all kinds of people. LMA, however, probably comes closest to being the most workable answer for most people.

Why move your muscles? What good does that do? After all, what you want to do is to cool off, to calm down, to stop your irritability. Jane says, "It's just the opposite of what I've been taught. As a girl, I remember distinctly being told to slow down or to calm down. Count to ten. Relax; take it easy. Stop getting upset."

Large Muscle Activity is just the opposite of what most readers of middle-class background tend to do. After a tough day down at the paper and people mill, most of us tend to plop our weary bodies in a chair, take a drink (alcohol is a depressant), and try to calm down, to slow our bodies down. This is just the opposite of LMA.

The facts, however, are overwhelmingly clear: Emotion, anger, or stress (call it what you like) prepares the body to move, to act physically, and to engage in muscle activity. These are physiological facts dimly recalled by most of us from some distant high-school or college physiology course. None of these facts are new, but people rarely recall them during the emotional heat of the typical working day.

What are these facts? What are the specific physiological responses of our bodies to anger/emotion/stress? Let's take a brief look at any basic physiology text. Bart and Taylor (1958) is a classic in this area. These authors state that the autonomic nervous system reacts to high emotion by the following:

Acceleration of the heart.
Mobilization of sugar from the liver.
Rise in blood pressure.
Diversion of blood from the skin. . .to the brain, the heart, and the contracting muscles.
Increased coagulation of blood.

Another author (Hilgard, Atkinson, & Atkinson, 1975) states additional changes:

Respiration becomes more rapid.
The motility of the gastrointestinal tract decreases or stops.

In addition, under high stress, there is a rise in serum cholesterol and blood fat (Rosenman & Friedman, 1974).

These changes are produced by a number of hormones, perhaps thirty different ones (adrenalin being the most well known), as well as by the activity of the pituitary, the hypothalamus, and so on. Briefly, the sympathetic aspect of the autonomous nervous system prepares the body for engaging in muscle activity by producing numerous changes, including the following:

1. Increasing the fuel in the blood that is required for muscle activity (oxygen, sugar, fats, and cholesterol).
2. Pumping this blood/fuel faster and at higher pressure.
3. Moving blood/fuel to those parts of the body needed for LMA, that is, the muscles, and removing blood/fuel from parts of the body not needed for LMA, that is, the digestive system.
4. Minimizing potential loss of blood in case of physical injury.

The sole purpose of these changes is to prepare the body to engage effectively in some kind of Large Muscle Activity. This is the old "fight or flight" reaction most of us recall learning about. Actually, under emotion/stress the body prepares to engage in any kind of LMA, not just fight or flight. This preparation is part of our genetic make-up. It has developed during the million-year history of human evolution. The reader will recall that this physiological preparation remains part of our genetic make-up solely because for most of those million years, LMA *was* the best response to emotion/stress. Engaging in LMA increased the chances of human survival.

Since your body automatically prepares you for LMA under stress, I suggest that you engage in LMA as soon as you are aware of your mounting stress. Engaging in LMA will reverse all those physiological changes. By moving your muscles you use up fuel in the blood, reduce your heart rate and blood pressure, and reverse all the rest of the physiological changes as well.

Most important is another change. Our emotions are also reversed. Just as LMA changes our bodies back to a former, more relaxed state (homeostasis), our emotions are modulated as well. We feel less anger—or less of whatever stressful emotion was originally aroused. The results are fast and clear-cut: *We feel better.*

How do you apply this? First of all, *at work*. There are at least five specific possibilities:

1. **WALK.**
2. **EXERCISES.**
3. **STRETCH.**
4. **ISOMETRICS.**
5. **SMALL MUSCLE ACTIVITY.**

Let's consider them in detail.

WALK

Walk anywhere. Walk down the hall. Walk back and forth across your office. Walk to the toilet (whether you have to use it or not). Walk down to the end of the building or to the other side of the plant. Walk up and down stairs. Walk.

Al is the head of an organization with a large physical plant stretched over several buildings. In the past, when he became annoyed with one of his subordinates, he would call the individual on the phone and ask the subordinate to come to his office. He would stew in his chair just waiting to pounce on him or her when he or she came in. After recognizing the physiological changes in his body, Al now does this: When he is angry at a subordinate, he gets up and walks out of his building down to the building where the subordinate works. He says sheepishly, "Most of the time, I almost hate to admit, by the time I get to the building the subordinate works in, I turn right around and come back. After the walk, all my steam is gone! If I still want to talk to the person, I go in, but always with a different perspective. I'm more able to listen to his point of view."

Don has also learned about LMA. Don has gotten into the habit of walking instead of using his buzzer. He doesn't buzz his secretary anymore but gets up from his desk, walks out to her desk, and walks back. He then gets the LMA instead of his secretary getting it. He also does this with his immediate subordinates and colleagues. He walks out to their nearby offices instead of calling them on the phone. Matt is a pacer. He paces back and forth in his office or out to his secretary down the hall. He used to be uncomfortable doing it until he realized how much his large muscles needed just that kind of release. Now he's comfortable pacing, laughs about it, and encourages others in the office to do it, too. In most jobs, walking is the most available form of LMA.

EXERCISES

Any kind of exercise will do as long as it gets those muscles moving. If you do the Royal Canadian Air Force exercise program (or the Royal Japanese or whatever), do some of the specific exercises shown.* Do push-ups or jumping jacks, run in place, or shadow box (hit that boss!). Do toe touches, squat thrusts, leg kicks, or side twisters (such names!). Do them right in your office—if you have one—or in the nearest other comfortable place you can find.

Jane is an elementary school principal. She reported this situation: "A parent came in who was quite angry: She was furious with the school, with her child's teachers, and with me. I wasn't prepared; I didn't know the situation. I had no documentation. I was caught unaware and really flipped under the attack. I then remembered LMA. I excused myself, went down the hall to a small closet, went inside, and did twenty jumping jacks. I caught my breath and went back completely restored. In less than ten minutes, I dealt with the parent comfortably, adequately, and to her satisfaction. It really works." Lyn has a private office, and he keeps a jump rope in his drawer. When things get tough, he takes off his jacket, pulls out the rope, and spends a minute or two jumping. Jumping rope is very vigorous, and it doesn't take too many jumps before his stress is lowered. Jack spends many hours in labor/management negotia-

* See the list of suggested readings for books on exercise.

tions. The time spent is tense and highly stressed. One day, he just couldn't take it anymore: He excused himself from the negotiating table and walked out of the room. Right outside the door, he did a number of push-ups. The release was great. His body was telling him that he had to move, and Jack responded to it.

Some organizations are recognizing the value of physical fitness and are providing gymnasiums right in the physical plant. If these exercise or release rooms are available, use them during the day for stress release not just for physical fitness.*

STRETCHING

Stretching the old body relieves tension and reduces some of the stress. It doesn't move as many muscles as walking or exercising, but it is often more socially acceptable. Stretch to the ceiling, stretch to one side, and stretch to the other side. Get up; get off your chair. Stretch and touch the floor (bend your knees if you have lower back trouble); stretch slowly; stretch faster. Get those muscles moving. This can

*Japanese industry has traditionally had daily exercise or gymnastic breaks for all employees. In these breaks, everyone, from the top executives on down, exercises together. Team cohesiveness, loyalty, productivity, and stress release are fostered by these group exercise programs.

American industry in recent years has shown a remarkable increase in awareness of the dollar and cents value of physical fitness for all employees. As an example, the American Association of Fitness Directors in Business and Industry has increased its membership from thirty-nine members in 1975 to over 815 members in 1979. There has been a parallel increase in industry expenditure for physical fitness laboratories, fitness testing, fitness programs and materials, and in capital investment in gymnasiums and exercise facilities. Some of the top names in American business reflect this trend: Xerox, Kimberly-Clark, Mobil, General Foods, and the like. Xerox alone has capital investments in excess of five million dollars in facilities for physical fitness. Yearly on going expenses for such programs are in the millions. Although these fitness programs primarily foster physical health values for employees, the stress release value (LMA) of physical exercise is often recognized and emphasized. Check the facilities available where you work.

sometimes be done while walking, too. Stretch regularly—at least every hour. Get in the habit of remembering to do at least this much LMA.

ISOMETRIC EXERCISES

These are nicely surreptitious forms of muscle activity to be used when you can't get up—when you can't even leave to go to the bathroom or to exercise. If you are in a conference with your boss and feel the stress rising, or if you are in a meeting you can't leave, these are the times for isometrics. In isometrics, we squeeze the muscles but do not move them (moving muscles is an isotonic exercise). Squeeze your hand or your abdomen tightly and release. Clasp your hands together tightly and pull your hands away from each other. Release and repeat. While sitting listening intently to the boss, alternately squeeze your buttocks tightly together and release them. You can do this a number of times, and he won't be able to see one bit of all that activity. In the dentist's chair, I clutch the arms of the chair tightly when the dentist starts drilling. I often clutch and release my hands as they grab the arm of the chair. This provides me with some physical release when I can't get up and run away (which I desperately have the urge to do—LMA again). Women during childbirth clutch on to stirrup-like holders in order to ease the pain of labor. This provides an isometric type of squeezing and releasing. Sometimes isometric activity is not enough. It just doesn't provide enough stress release, because those large muscles don't move. Use it anyway as a temporary measure until you can get up and walk or get to your more private exercise place.

SMALLER MUSCLE ACTIVITIES

In other situations where we are unable to move or are uncomfortable about getting up to walk or to exercise, opportunities exist for moving smaller muscles. These, like isometrics, may provide sufficient stress release or may be used just to hold us over until we can get up and move our large muscles. Under a table or desk, your feet won't be seen if you wiggle them. You can also fidget with something or wiggle other various parts of your body. Scribbling or doodling on paper gives us another small muscle release, and many people use it to release the stress of boredom or other emotions while they are physically tied to a chair. I used to smoke a pipe and spent an inordinately large amount of time fidgeting with it—biting on the bit, poking in the bowl, reaming and cleaning and using pipe cleaners. I got in all kinds of hand activity. All these provided some small kind of muscle release. I have also heard of a police department that recognized the stress that builds up in their police officers who have to sit for many hours in a patrol car. These police officers were each given a small, spring-loaded hand exerciser. You've probably seen them in gyms or physical fitness stores. You squeeze it against the spring; it springs open again; and you squeeze it again. Patrol officers could wile away their boring or tense waiting time sitting in a patrol car by getting some small muscle release. The results were dramatic: less tension, less emotional difficulties or conflict, and less problems with patrol officers letting off steam or irritating members of the public. And, as I understand it, even their wives found them easier to live with. And of course they must have developed some pretty strong hand muscles! Even *small* muscle release can affect our emotions and reduce our stress.

The second way we apply LMA is on a regular, routine basis. In addition to using LMA immediately as your stress/ anger rises at work, the LMA principle can be applied routinely and regularly by engaging in LMA four, five, or more times per week, thirty minutes to one hour each time. Engaging regularly and routinely in LMA considerably enhances its values: Regular LMA provides for the release of stress that accumulated daily. If your brain, while under stress, forgets to remind you to move your muscles at work, routine LMA takes care of that slip. If you can't get out of the work situation all day, even for a short walk, regular LMA takes care of that, too. More significantly, routinely scheduled LMA serves as a preventative mechanism for stress. LMA results in your feeling better emotionally. This emotional glow and the relaxation that accompanies it will last for hours. Mary and her husband go for vigorous walks first thing every morning. They do it together because it's more enjoyable and because they need to support each other in order to do it regularly. Mary says, "After our walk we feel great. We're more awake and alert, more ready to start the day, and that good feeling lasts almost all day." Don walks vigorously during his lunch hour. Besides lowering his accumulated morning stress, he feels better in the afternoons and gets less up tight, less angry, and less frustrated. Jack plays tennis or handball or gets a workout in the gym every day after leaving work. He does this before he enters the family scene. Jack says that the good feeling carries over when he gets home. He deals with the children more calmly, is more loving with his wife, and is less prone to anger. Routine LMA is a preventative.

What kinds of LMA can be used for positive stress release four, five, or six times per week? A whole variety of possibilities follow:

Walking, of course.
Exercises, as previously mentioned.
Running, jogging, biking, or swimming—much has been written on this.
Sports of all kinds.
An exercycle in your home or office.
Jumping rope.
Dancing—aerobic, folk, jazzercise, and the like.
Gardening—chopping weeds or pushing the mower.
Housework—including waxing the car or boat.
And last but not least—sex.

The emotional reaction after routine LMA is over-whelmingly positive. When I ask people who engage in regular LMA how they feel afterwards, the response is the same. They almost always, in fact, use identical words. They answer, "I feel great." No matter what the physical activity, the emotional reaction is positive. Check it out yourself. Go through the above list. Recall the last time you engaged in regular LMA—not just once or twice, but regularly—four to five times per week. How do you recall feeling afterwards?

See if you can also recall the preventative value. Did your regular LMA sustain you for many hours afterwards in a calmer emotional mood? Were you less irritable, less disturbed by frustration? Were you more able to cope with stressful situations by being more pleasant and more rational? People who self-monitor their reactions (see Section 1) affirm this response over and over again. Check it out yourself.

As effective as LMA is, it's of no use if we don't do it. We have seen that for most of us, our typical (and even trained) reactions are not in the direction of muscle activity. Supposedly, Mark Twain said, "When I feel the urge for physical activity, I go to bed until the urge goes away." My experience leads me to believe that there are many Mark Twains reading this book. This is particularly true of well-educated individuals, persons with managerial responsibility, working mothers, and the like. Are you emulating Mark Twain?

What further aggravates the problem of applying LMA is the issue raised in Chapter 2. In that chapter, the emphasis was that under higher levels of stress, we do not think very well (if at all). We don't think of alternatives. We don't remember to walk or to move our muscles at the times when we need to do it the most! Therefore we need all the memory help we can get to recall LMA when that stress level is rising on the job. In order to help us remember to use LMA, let's look in more detail at the rationale behind the technique. Specifically, what happens to our bodies when anger and stress rise? I'll include some studies, some legends, and some personal experiences. All of the following is offered as specific help for both your memory processes and your ingrained Mark Twain tendencies.

What are the physiological changes accompanying emotion/anger/stress? Remember that the fuel (oxygen, sugar, and fats) for LMA increases in the blood. Perhaps you remember from that high-school course that oxygen combines with sugar (or fat in a more complicated fashion) and that the result is muscle energy and waste products. Perhaps you have heard more recently how certain fats, especially cholesterol, increase under high stress. A classic research study on cholesterol and stress was done by Rosenman and Friedman (1974). They studied accountants. The cholesterol level of a group of accountants was measured once a month. Their diet was the same each month and was controlled in the study. Most of the year, the blood cholesterol of the accountants remained level. Before income tax time, however, the blood cholesterol of these accountants shot up and remained that way for several months. That rigid old genetic intelligence told the bodies of these accountants under the stress of income taxes to prepare for LMA. Their bodies did this by shooting fuel for muscle activity into their blood. Around May or so the cholesterol level lowered. It was no longer needed for LMA. Remember that this also happens to your blood under high anger/stress.

Remember that the blood pumps faster under higher pressure. In order to make those muscles move, that fuel must get to the muscles (and to the heart and brain). So the cardiovascular system pumps it out there faster and under higher pressure. If you've ever had your blood pressure taken and it was too high, the physician probably told you to relax. If you did relax, the pressure decreased. I have a dramatic example of this from my own personal experience.

My blood pressure for some time was mildly high. It ranged around 140/92. I had it taken one morning and then went swimming at the "Y." I swam for about thirty minutes— continuous lap swimming. On the way out, I noticed that they were doing blood pressure checks in the gym. I got in line and had my pressure checked. I was astounded to discover that my blood pressure had dropped to a very low 120/70! I was still so incredulous when I got home and told my wife that we hopped in the car, went back to the "Y," and had it taken again by another person. It was still dramatically low!

Heart rate also increases under high emotion. How sharply it rises when we are angry was illustrated in a research study of an executive/manager who was having his heart monitored while at work. Research scientists have developed neat little miniaturized instruments that do this. The average rate at which the heart pumps while at rest (no stress) is about 70 beats per minute. This man walked up stairs for exercise. The monitor showed an increase to 120 beats per minute. This is not unusual: The increase in fuel pumping is needed for LMA. But under anger, when our executive had an argument with his secretary, his heart rate increased to 160 beats per minute. This was considerably higher than that needed for walking up stairs. Remember that when you are angry, that beautiful mechanism, your body, pumps blood at a higher rate through your body.

Heart rate also accelerates under the stressful emotion of fear. Perhaps you recall experiencing your heart rate accelerate when you are afraid. During World War II, 4,604 fliers were studied (Shaffer, 1947). They were asked the question, "During combat missions, what did you feel?" Eighty percent of these combat fliers answered, "A pounding heart and rapid pulse." Again, the body response to stress is to pump blood faster out to those muscles.

Remember that the blood goes to the parts of the body needed for LMA and is removed from those parts not needed for LMA. There are some easy ways to remember this. First of all, everyone has recognized, under anger/ stress, a tenseness in his or her muscles. Those muscles want to move. When angered or stressed, we have an uncontrollable need to get up or to act—perhaps to pace or even to hit out physically. The fuel is shooting out to the muscles; all systems are "go," and we can feel it. The fliers that Shaffer studied recognized this often. Eighty-three percent of them reported "muscles very tense" during combat missions.

At the same time that the muscular system is "go," the digestive system is "stop." In order to make your muscles move, you don't need to digest food. The digestive system "decreases in motility." This wrecks digestive havoc with those of us who were brought up by Jewish mothers (of course you don't have to be Jewish to be a Jewish Mother). Jewish mothers (Italian, etc.) think that food is the answer to everything. When you are hungry, eat; when you aren't hungry, eat anyway. Eat when you are tired, eat when you are weary—eat especially when you are upset or under stress. Shove the bottle or breast at the baby: The baby stops crying. But those of us who do eat under stress realize the uncomfortable consequences: Our digestive system is just not working. All that food just sits there—undigested. The result is gas, a heavy feeling in the stomach, and considerable discomfort. All of you brought up by Jewish mothers will recognize this reaction. The digestive system is not needed for muscle activity. Some of you perhaps recall some time in your life when you were under such severe stress (possibly during combat) that your bladder and bowels emptied. The contents of that part of the digestive system just got in the way of LMA. In James Fixx's book on running (1977), he describes an incident where a woman runner under the severe muscle activity of long distance running actually had diarrhea while running! He writes that she kept on running; the diarrhea was not a medical problem. The undigested food in her system just wasn't needed for LMA.

Another way to remember what's happening to your digestive system under stress is by remembering a famous legend about an ancient Chinese lie detection technique. The ancient Chinese knew that the saliva in the mouth stops flowing under high stress. The saliva is, of course, part of our "unnecessary" digestive system. Often when I give talks to large audiences, I feel my own stressful reaction as dryness in my mouth. I ask for water at the podium because I constantly feel thirsty—of course, it's only my high stress! If the ancient Chinese wanted to test whether someone was lying, they gave the person an astringent herb to chew on. The inquisitor then had the chewer spit out those leaves on a special ceremonial plate. If the leaves were wet, the man was considered not under high stress and was freed. If the leaves were dry, off with his head! I don't recommend using this technique with your subordinates or your children, but it may help you to remember what's happening to your body every time you get stressed.

Remember too, that in order to prevent loss of blood from an injury, blood leaves the skin; it also coagulates faster. Throughout most of the million years of human history, LMA response considerably increased the chances of physical injury. The primary survival concern was to prevent loss of blood. The body evolved mechanisms to do just that. Every time you are angry/stressful, capillaries in your skin contract, so that less blood is available at the skin. Paleness of the body (not always of the face) indicates this. To be doubly safe, the body also reduces loss of blood by increasing the coagulability of the blood. These blood clotting elements have been aptly called "emergency sealants." This body change is intimately related to heart disease. We all have heard of someone who has survived a heart attack and who is now taking some drug to "thin out his or her blood." This obviously prevents that "emergency sealant" from sticking to the inside of the arteries, clogging them up, and eventually causing a heart attack or stroke. Remember that when you experience high stress, your blood gets thicker, stickier, and more ready to clog. It does this as part of that million-year evolvement—to save your life. This, of course, explains a tie-in between heart disease and stress, and understanding this could also save your life.

So, in summary, consider a technique you can use often and almost anywhere—one that works for many people and one that is both direct and fast. Excuse the brief excursion into physiology, but its purpose was solely to aid your use of the technique. None of this is really new to you. I hope, however, that your knowledge is now clearer on the subject and that you understand the rationale for my recommending the technique. All this may well result in your willingness to experiment with LMA. Add it to your repertoire of stress- and emotion-lowering techniques. You may well be surprised by its power in breaking old stress patterns!

RECALL REMINDER

7

DON'T TALK— WALK!

In your work situation, list the places you can walk to or those where you can stretch or do exercises to lower your stress:

_____

_____

_____

If you do not do routine LMA now, what muscle activities have you done in the past that you might consider starting again on a regular basis?

_____

_____

_____

List some new LMA possibilities you have never tried but might like to begin to do on a regular basis:

_____

_____

_____

THE DO-NUT

In reading through Part One, you may have recognized some of your own methods of coping with anger/dissatisfaction. Those put-downs, dumping on your family, or accumulating anger/dissatisfaction in your body may be techniques you are now ready to give up. Or there may be other anger behaviors and reactions—not described—that you dislike in yourself. Possibly you've decided that anger/dissatisfaction in general is nonproductive. You may be tired of your own anger and unhappy with its effect on the quality of your life or on the people around you. Perhaps you've had enough of it, and you want to handle yourself and other people differently. Possibly, too, as you review your own anger situations from Chapter 4, you may recognize a recurrent pattern in your life. You may be ready to stop "playing the same old anger tapes." You may have someone at work (or at home) you would like to react to more positively and more productively.

Whatever your reasons for wanting to become less angry, this chapter offers you a tool that can help you do just that. It is a simple but an extremely powerful one. Basically, the tool offered here is a different way of looking at or understanding anger. The tool is called the Do-nut (see Figure 8–1). The Do-nut is a graphic way of illustrating that *all anger is a cover-up.*

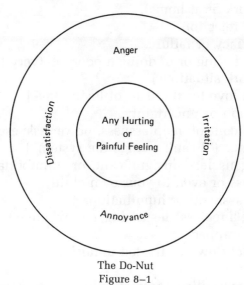

The Do-Nut
Figure 8–1

Anger is used to cover up other feelings—feelings that may be too painful for us to face or to cope with. Anger covers these feelings so effectively that we often don't even feel those underlying feelings while we are angry. What the Do-nut says is that anger is an emotion that we experience on the outside (of the Do-nut) and that underneath (inside, in the hole of the Do-nut) are a host of other feelings—feelings that hurt, are painful, or are uncomfortable. Anger then covers up and hides these more painful feelings from us. Anger is a way of coping with hurt and pain—a mechanism, if you like, that is available to us to use when certain feelings hurt too much. While we are angry, we don't feel (are not aware of) those hurting, uncomfortable feelings.

Let's take a look at what feelings can hurt so much or can be so uncomfortable that we often turn them into anger in order not to feel them. There are a host of painful, uncomfortable feelings, such as the following:

Rejection or being ignored (probably by someone close to us).

Not being recognized, appreciated, or understood (at work or at home).

Fear of rejection.

Inadequacy or failure.

Fear of failing or of doing a poor job (very frequent in work situations).

Loss of love (or the fear of losing love).

Confusion or uncertainty.

Loss of control, helplessness, powerlessness, or impotence ("I can't change the system").

Feeling useless, insignificant, or unimportant (to the boss or even to your own child).

Embarrassment or humiliation.

Feeling hopeless, despairing, overwhelmed, worthless, or trapped.

Being let down or treated unfairly.

Guilt.

Loss of masculinity or femininity (however we define it).

Insecurity (job, financial fears).

Any other fears (losing our promotion, our job, or our life).

Physical pain (or fear of pain).

Any other uncomfortable, painful feeling.

Let's consider in detail a number of job situations where we get angry (see Chapter 4) and see how this list of feelings from inside the do-nut can help us to understand the reasons for our anger.

In Chapter 4, we mentioned Ted. Remember that Ted was angry because a decision had been made affecting his work without anyone consulting with him or asking for his point of view. Underneath, inside the Do-nut, Ted probably felt ignored or rejected; more certainly, he felt unrecognized or unimportant. If these feelings hurt too much, Ted could (as he did) turn them into anger.

Joan, you will recall, was blamed for some problem she didn't create. She's angry at her boss. Inside her Do-nut, there are probably hurt feelings of being blamed, unrecognized, and misunderstood, as well as feelings of unfairness. Perhaps there is even a feeling of rejection because the boss didn't even bother checking with her. Any one of these (or a combination of them) could be the cause of her anger.

We noted that one source of anger arose out of our concerns for competently accomplishing our jobs. This anger/dissatisfaction was especially noted when job pressures rise, when unreasonable demands are placed on us, or when heavy deadlines exist. In these kinds of situations, most people identify underlying feelings as a concern over failing or being inadequate. These are very typical work-related underlying feelings—the fear of failing or of doing a poor job. Sometimes individuals report other painful job feelings inside their Do-nuts—feeling unrecognized, not appreciated, unimportant, and the like. Any of these could readily be turned into anger/dissatisfaction.

Individuals who are managers or supervisors report a number of underlying painful feelings that explain their anger. Subordinates do not respond to supervision, do not change after much effort to get them to change, do not follow through on instructions, do not perform properly, and so on. Underneath, inside the Do-nut, the manager has feelings of being ignored or rejected, feelings of failing as a manager ("I tried to change him and failed"), and concern over the task not being accomplished (fear of failing again). Any of these feelings or any combination of them can hurt enough for us to cover them up and turn them into anger.

Underlying painful feelings can be aroused in our family situations quite readily. Loss of love or the fear of losing love (or a loved one) can be a very painful feeling. Take the case of the mother whose child was lost all day. She was in tears until the doorbell rang and the policeman entered with the lost child. What did she do upon getting the child back? Beat the hell out of him, of course. "How could you cause me such pain, such fear?" She turned her fear of losing her child (and possibly some guilt as well) into furious anger and let it loose on the child who "caused" her pain. Losing love or the fear of losing love can be extremely painful and can also be readily covered up with anger. Widows and others who have lost loved ones can recognize this source of their anger.

Any of the underlying feelings listed works the same way. These feelings lie underneath our outward anger. And anger so effectively covers up those hurting feelings underneath that, typically, all we feel is the anger. The anger mechanism has been successful—so successful that we don't feel at all what's hurting underneath.

Consider your own anger/dissatisfaction situations (refer to page 80). Can you identify the underlying feelings? Check out the list of possible hurting or painful feelings. It might help to discuss this with a friend or spouse or partner; together, you might find it easier to identify those painful feelings. Even when angry at a strange driver who shoots in front of us on the freeway, we can identify underlying feelings. Our underlying fear of being hurt or our underlying feeling of powerlessness are typically the feelings we hide under our anger. If this happened while driving home after a particularly trying day at work where other hurts and fears were aroused, we can readily see the source of our anger. It is this combination of painful feelings that we trigger into anger and let loose on that "damned" driver.

Some people identify certain feelings or patterns of feelings that seem to explain most of their anger. Often, fear of inadequacy, of failing, or of doing a poor job can be especially painful. I discovered that feeling helpless or powerless is particularly hurtful to me. Several times in my life I have stayed in very bad situations, trying desperately to produce change when change was impossible. I have done this rather than allow myself to feel helpless, inadequate, or powerless. In these situations, I developed a great deal of anger rather than face what, for me, were and are especially painful feelings.

What underlying feelings are particularly significant to you because they hurt too much or are too painful?

After you have been able to identify the underlying feelings covering up your anger, how can this help you become less angry? How specifically can you use the Do-nut to reduce your anger? The steps in accomplishing this are the following:

> **STEP 1:** First of all, decide that you want to become less angry in general, in a specific repetitive situation, or in a special relationship (boss, customer, spouse, etc.).
>
> **STEP 2:** Accept the Do-nut as a 100% explanation of anger. It is imperative to do this. Otherwise you will allow yourself a cop-out. Try it out, at least for several weeks.
>
> **STEP 3:** The very next time you are angry/dissatisfied with your boss, that customer or co-worker, or your spouse, bring down your emotional temperature so that you become more capable of thinking rationally. Use LMA or any other technique in this book or in your repertoire of successful emotion-lowering techniques.
>
> **STEP 4:** Then, and only then, apply the Do-nut by seeking the underlying hurt and pain.
>
> **STEP 5:** At the next recurrence or possible recurrence, institute Steps 1 through 4. Recall the Do-nut. This may not prevent the anger, but it usually reduces how long you remain angry.

Individuals report that after several repetitions of the above five steps, either of two changes takes place: (1) They do not become angry/dissatisfied in these situations, or (2) their anger lasts only momentarily. It quickly dissipates, and reasonableness, understanding, and/or love replace it.

Give it a try. It works!

The Do-nut has two other powerful uses in helping you to break the pattern of dissatisfaction in your life. The second use of the Do-nut is in confrontation. If you decide to confront the person you are angry or dissatisfied with, the Do-nut provides you with an especially valuable tool to do just that. The Do-nut provides you with a way of letting the other person know how you feel—not the anger, but the underlying feelings. Sometimes we let the person know how we feel by letting loose the outside of the Do-nut (the anger) on that person. We may even start out calmly by saying, "What you did makes me angry." This doesn't always go over too well. Sometimes, when we do this we get angry all over again, and an argument or fight ensues.

The Do-nut provides you with an alternative means of communication. After you have used the Do-nut, you now understand your underlying hurt. This second use of the Do-nut recommends that you tell the person not of your anger but of your hurt (the inside of your Do-nut).

Generally, if we let another person know that we are hurting or in pain, the most typical reaction is a sympathetic one. People want to comfort us. They offer an empathetic, compassionate response. The approach is to share that hurt. Look within the Do-nut; discover what your underlying hurts, pains, and discomforts are (see the list on page 80); and then tell the other person what they are. In most relationships, you can expect a sympathetic response. The response is bound to be a better one than if you turn the hurt into anger and then express the anger.

Sometimes it appears risky to let the other person know we are hurting. We feel vulnerable. We are afraid that the other person will hurt us more, that it will be used against us or held against us. When we think about the persons most likely to do this, the boss is frequently mentioned. If we let him or her know that we are hurting—for example, "I'm confused and not sure how to cope with this" or even, "I feel inadequate and I'm not sure I can handle that job"—this might be held against us at promotion or evaluation time. Other people who would be risky to share hurt with might be persons considered to be malicious gossips or people we are in competition with at work.

It is considerably less risky to share hurt with someone who cares for you or has affection or love for you. We share hurting feelings more easily, then, with family and intimate friends and perhaps less readily with supervisors or other people at work.

Surprisingly, as people have applied the Do-nut in their work situations, many of them have discovered that there is a large fund of compassion in the people we work with—our supervisors, subordinates, customers, and clients. In most cases, we have not even begun to tap those caring, concerned feelings because instead, we have turned our hurt into anger. It is undoubtedly risky, but the effort might be worth it. Often, by sharing our hurts, we discover that the other person hurts, too. And this can be a real eye-opener—to discover, for example, where your boss hurts and what worries him. Sharing of hurt often opens up communication: We understand the other guy better, and he understands us. At the least, sometimes we just get "to cry on each other's shoulders," and that, too, is comforting and human. A boss who knows you are hurting has a wonderful opportunity to share his previous experience in a way to help you grow. "I know you are hurting; I was there once, too. I've gotten through it. You can too." Or even, "Tell me your fears and inadequacies. My job is to help you overcome them." Try this out with your subordinates!

One last comment on sharing hurt and pain. At times, you may choose to let another person know the inside of your Do-nut, and they may respond with "I don't care," "Too bad," or some other negative response. According to the all-useful Do-nut again, the explanation is clear: They are hurting. You are hurting, but they are also hurting—so much so that they cannot respond to your hurt with compassion. You have several alternatives here. Rather than get into a battle, you could separate and try again later when the other individual is experiencing less pain. Or you may be able to say to yourself, "I'm hurting, but he's hurting, too." If you care enough or feel strong enough, you can temporarily set aside your own hurt. An excellent approach to helping others in pain is to listen (Gordon, 1970). This typically brings down the angry person's emotional temperature (see chapter 9 on venting). You can usually do this more readily with spouses or children, because your care for them is clear. But try it on your boss, or on a customer, a taxpayer, a student, or the like. You may well be surprised at how you can lower someone's emotional temperature sufficiently so that he or she becomes capable of listening to where you are coming from.

The third use of the Do-nut is to help you deal with angry people. If someone lashes out at us, our most typical response is to get defensive and to attack back. If you tire of this reaction in yourself, you can use the Do-nut to prevent yourself from getting angry in turn. How do you do that? Well, the basic idea of the Do-nut holds for the other person as well as for you. Whenever you are angry, the Do-nut says that you are hurting underneath. When the other guy is angry or attacking or complaining, it must mean that he is hurting, too. It may seem a bit difficult to do, but while he or she is lashing out at you, keep the Do-nut in mind—remember that the person is hurting. Some individuals find it helps to "center" on the Do-nut. Typically, if you don't get defensive and attack back, the attacking person vents all his or her anger and then runs down on anger. Soon he or she starts expressing the inside of his or her Do-nut—the underlying hurt. You can then tell where he or she is coming from and understand the feelings. Possibly, you may even sympathize with the person, even though he or she started out attacking you. I'm sure that all of us have had an experience when someone started out attacking us, and we didn't attack him or her in turn. If we just listened instead, soon the anger gave way, and the person expressed his or her hurts, feelings of injustice, or pain. Use the Do-nut to help you to do this with angry people, and you won't get as defensive or feel as hurt yourself.

In summary, you now have a tool to help you become less angry. Whether you decide to remain angry or to give anger up is your decision. Use your self-monitoring data to decide whether anger/dissatisfaction raises your stress level too high. You may decide you'd rather be angry. You may enjoy your anger! You may decide, as some people have, that the underlying hurt feelings are still more painful than getting angry, with its consequences (see chapter 15, Human Pain). The Do-nut cannot remove your pain, but it can make it more tolerable. If you choose to retain your anger, you still have other techniques in this book to lower your stress to levels that are more acceptable to you. Review some of them. And then there is the ultimate force that ameliorates much of our pain—the slow passage of time. Consider the alternatives. You do have choices.

RECALL REMINDER

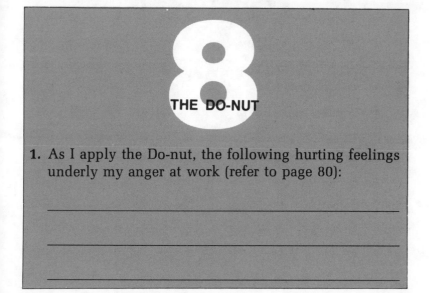

8

THE DO-NUT

1. As I apply the Do-nut, the following hurting feelings underly my anger at work (refer to page 80):

_____

_____

_____

2. The following hurting feelings underly my anger elsewhere (refer again to page 80):

_____

_____

_____

3. The next time I get angry at_____, I
will try to use the Do-nut to reduce my anger.

TALKING TO OTHERS

The priest, the psychologist, and the confidant: All hold in common a unique ability to listen and to listen well. Traditionally, a good listener has always been a source of help in times of stress.

This chapter will take a look at the technique of venting our feelings, at what makes it work for us, and at who we can use to get this kind of stress release.

All of us have discovered at some point in our lives the powerful release that comes from letting it all out. However we describe it—as a venting of emotion, as a public release of inner feelings, as a catharsis—the experience is valuable for stress release. The quality of this venting is, however, crucial. There are two kinds of venting of feelings that we are not considering in this chapter. We are not considering here any release of feelings that puts down the listener as we take out our anger/stress on that person (that was discussed in Chapter 4). That can feel like a release, but as we have noted, it creates problems for us, is at best temporary, and is not a true release. The second kind of release not being considered here is the approach that requires finding someone who has the same feeling we do and venting to them in order to find agreement or an ally. For example, after we've been criticized by the boss, we can seek out someone who also feels put upon by the boss and vent our anger/dissatisfaction to them. We share the same feelings, and we have a hot time hating the boss together. When we do that, we merely feed our stress; it often spirals higher and higher, and we do nothing or little to lower it. Finding someone who hates the same person (or people) we do is *not* the cathartic release we are talking about in this chapter. It's not recommended anywhere in this book: You know how to do it anyway and don't need any help from me.

In this chapter, we are concerned with an approach that requires very special behaviors on the part of the listener. Most people, as they think about the kind of person who has helped them in the past, want the following reactions in the listener:

Someone who will listen.

Someone who will not be judgmental: "You shouldn't have done that," or, just as bad, "That was great."

Someone who will show interest, verbally or nonverbally (such as the psychologist's grunt, "Uhuh," accompanied by a head nod).

Someone who will be confidential (no gossip; won't use it to shaft you or embarrass you).

Someone who understands and cares.

Someone with feelings of empathy and compassion (a generally sympathetic attitude).

When we get this kind of listening, the results are often like magic: Our emotions can take a 180° turn. It's another way of bringing us down from that emotion/stress peak (see Figure 9–1).

We usually feel better; we even have a sense of relief. We feel unburdened, lighter. We often feel less alone; there

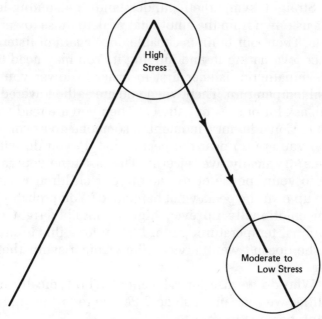

Lowering Our Emotional Temperature
Figure 9–1

is less of a feeling of being wrong, bad, or angry. Sometimes too we gain in clarity, because as we climb down the right side of the peak (Figure 9–1), our stress lowers to levels where our brains are operating at full swing again (refer to Chapter 2). We can think again and often begin doing just that.

Sometimes, when we consider the kind of person who has helped us in the past, some people report that someone acted as a sounding board for them, pointed out things they could not see, or gave advice or suggestions. However, not everyone wants these reactions in a listener. Some of us do; many of us do not. Decide what you want, and then seek out the person who can best help you. Remember, too (again from Chapter 2), that if you want advice, you will not be responsive to it until you have lowered your stress/emotion to more reasonable levels (see Figure 9–1 again).

Straight, sympathetic, understanding listening is what pulls us down from the emotional peak to those lower stress levels. Then, our brain is capable once again of listening to advice, evaluating it, and judging it. You may need to seek the sympathetic listener first in order to lower your emotional temperature. Then when you are at the lowered stress level, ask for or seek out advice. Then you are ready to deal with it. Consider for a moment: If someone gives you advice when you are up near the peak, what do you do with that advice? Typically, we reject it. The last time you gave advice to your spouse or to one of your children when they were up near the peak, what happened? You probably drove them emotionally up even higher, possibly right off the emotional temperature graph! I have done this to my wife, but she doesn't want advice. She wants a sympathetic listener.

Who do we use for a listener? Who typically has the qualities we seek in a listener? People report using the following persons to vent to:

Spouses.
Other intimates and friends.
Coworkers or colleagues.
Peers, either in the work situation or elsewhere.
Strangers or others.

Many people report using their spouses for this venting, sharing with their spouses, and getting the supportive response without advice or recommendation. Many men do this, and it can be most helpful in times of stress.

Recently I have become aware (as have many men) of a strong tendency in myself to use my wife for this and not to use other men to share feelings with. Many men have become aware of a similar tendency to express feelings much more easily to women than to other men. Men share activities, work, hobbies, sports, and the like with other men, but they do not share feelings as easily with other men. This is mainly a question of comfort. Sharing feelings with men can be cultivated and practiced. It can be a powerful ally in times of stress.

I encourage you to find individuals at work who can be sympathetic listeners. The kind of person who at times can be most understanding is someone in a peer position. Peers can especially appreciate what you are experiencing since they are experiencing it, too. If you want advice, they are more likely to be helpful here than your spouse. It is not necessary that the peer work where you work. He or she may be many miles away. Perhaps you met him or her at a convention or meeting and discovered the similarity of your responsibilities and job pressures. Call him or her on the phone if this is the only way. In large organizations, state and nationwide, parallel positions exist in large numbers. Very often, the organization pulls together persons in the same position for a meeting or conference. This is the time to make contact with peers. Ask if you can call them and use them for this listening purpose. Offer yourself as a listener. Let's make this venting process more effective and more usable by coming out in the open with it. Occasionally I find someone who can use his or her boss for this type of venting. This is obviously a very effective and helpful supervisory relationship. This also has possibilities you might want to explore with your boss or with your subordinates.

There are times when the person who is normally a good listener for you is just unable to offer you the right reactions you want in a listener. Right now, he or she is unable to show interest or feel compassion. He or she is not capable of understanding you. He or she just can't listen to you. When things inside ourselves are too strong, we listen to them and cannot listen to the outside world. Possibly you have chosen a time when he or she is at some emotional peak of his or her own (see Figure 9–1). Or perhaps, according to the Do-nut (see Chapter 8), he or she is experiencing some inner pain or hurt.

If, in fact, your listener responds with anger, you can automatically assume that he or she is hurting. Perhaps, then, you may be willing (able) to set aside your own stress and listen to him or her instead. You may find that you are unable to do this. Your stress level is just too high. You might then gently and kindly take leave of the person and seek out some other good listener (or some other technique). Sometimes, however, listening to someone else actually helps you with your stress. Your problem/worries no longer seem so important when you have heard the pain and problems of your "listener." Remember Figure 9–1 and the Do-nut (Chapter 8). Your listener may just be up there emotionally. Do not expect that your spouse or friend or peer can always be emotionally ready for you. Each has feelings and stress too.

How do you find someone to talk to if you don't have anyone? There are traditional roles in society in which people listen. There is, of course, the clergyman/rabbi/priest, and many of these individuals nowadays are additionally trained in counseling skills. There are, in addition, other professionals in our society trained to do this. Some people, I understand, even go to psychologists for this purpose. There are, too, other traditional roles—the bartender, the hairdresser. Some people have told me that they talk to their dogs and get the right response (don't knock it if it works). Some people use journal writing very effectively for venting or expressing their feelings. Some people report that they can, at times, even listen to themselves, using a thinking or talking out loud process that works for them. Any of these might work for you.

If you are the kind of person who generally does not publicly disclose your feelings and personal life, you may be uncomfortable doing this the first time. Like many things, it does become a lot easier the more you do it. I remember when I was recently divorced. I was embarrassed by the whole thing; I felt humiliated and ashamed. In addition, I felt a sense of failure and inadequacy. I kept it all to myself and didn't share it with all those people out there who wouldn't understand. One day, I happened to hear my lawyer's secretary talk about her divorce. This helped free me to share my feelings (to a woman, of course). But it became easier to talk about it, and then I started talking about my divorce almost everywhere I went (well, not everywhere). I discovered all sorts of people who had been divorced, were where I was, or had been there—all kinds of people who now understood me and my feelings. That whole world out there changed from being a source of stress to becoming a relief for my stress. Very powerful! Take some courage. The first time is the hardest. give it a try!

RECALL REMINDER

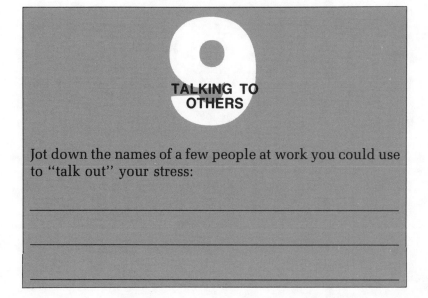

TALKING TO OTHERS

Jot down the names of a few people at work you could use to "talk out" your stress:

_____

_____

I would like to offer myself as a listener to the following
people (and will so inform them):

_____

_____

_____

SLOW DOWN

Think for a moment about the following questions related to your pace, your speed:

Do you find that you automatically speed up when there's more work to be done?

Do you feel that the only way you'll get all your work accomplished is to hurry it up and to work faster?

Or do you find that you work best with the pressure of a deadline hanging over your head? It's more exciting that way—being busy and stimulated?

Do you work fast because you are convinced it's part of your job, necessary for your competence, or required for your success?

Or do you often find yourself doing (or trying to do) two or three things at once? Is it exciting to have several persons trying to get your attention at the same time?

Do you feel that there's never enough time to get it all done?

Or are you the kind of person who speeds up almost all the time—hurry up; let's get it finished. Why the rush? To get it done, to accomplish it, to get rid of it. After all, there's always something else waiting to be done—in fact, a long list of things. So rush. Hurry. Get with it. Preoccupation with getting it done, over with, to the end. But there is no end. No end of jobs, tasks, and responsibilities. No rest for the weary. No peace or calm. High stress.

If any of the above fast-pace reactions are yours, you will probably find the premise of this chapter difficult to accept. The point of view offered here is that slowing down our pace can, at times, actually produce a higher level of productivity than the speeded up, accelerated pace described above.

One of the most persistent myths regarding our work behavior emphasizes speeding up as the appropriate response to any increase in tasks, in responsibilities, or in problems.

Somehow speed seems to be a preoccupation in our society. We race cars, boats, and bicycles; in fact, we race anything we can get our hands on, even our own bodies. We race from place to place and from activity to activity. We see the fast worker as the best worker. Fast = Efficient = Best. If you get done first, you're smarter. If you are slow, you are stupid, inept, or a procrastinator.

Those of us who rush (either intentionally or otherwise) recognize the stressful consequences. Rushing emphasizes getting it done, not the quality of the product. When we rush, our eye is on the goal, not on the process of achieving it. We don't enjoy the process. By pushing for the goal, we can easily stumble along the way and bump into something (and some of us do that quite literally).

When we rush, anything that slows us down as an obstacle arouses our ire and impatience. It prevents us from moving. During my most severe rushing behavior (and I used to be a real first-class hurrier), I viewed people in the world as either facilitators or blockers. They either got in my way or helped me. There were no other alternatives. Since all of us inevitably face blockers, the daily tasks of the rusher are inevitably filled with strife—the strife of mini-failures. All day long, there are obstacles, blocks, and interferences. All day long, our adrenaline (and all those other stress hormones) is running high. A fast pace shoots up our emotions, our anger/stress. We are bound to be impatient—impatient with anything or anyone that slows down our pace, gets in the way, or doesn't move as fast as we do. And this increases our stress even further. We deliberately set up for ourselves a multitude of inevitable mini-failures, such as the following:

The person who doesn't understand.
The person who doesn't obey.
The one who raises questions.
The person who disagrees.
The person who has his own needs and feelings.
The person who does things slowly or at a calmer pace.
Anyone who is doing his or her own thing and won't
    attend to us.

Someone once said to me in a stress seminar, "I wouldn't have any stress at all if the rest of the world would behave the way I want it to!" And the rest of the world can be just about anyone, especially people close to us: our co-workers and colleagues; our subordinates or bosses; our own children and spouses; other drivers on the streets; sales persons, clerks, cashiers, and tellers handling the lines in front of us.

Whenever we rush, too, any period of inevitable waiting becomes a painful experience—waiting in line, waiting for the car in front of you, waiting for the person behind the counter to get to you, waiting for someone to answer the phone, waiting to get to the door.

Acceleration, too, can often become pervasive. It spills over into all areas of our life. We don't turn it off when we get home from work. We eat fast, drive fast, and talk fast. We play fast, we relate to others in a fast manner, and we make love fast.

Speed, too, interferes with the concept of single-mindedness and with the ability to concentrate, and to focus. We go so fast that we are always one step ahead. We are rarely in the here and now. We can't give fully of ourselves to one situation, one problem, or one person. Our mind races ahead to the next situation, problem, or person. We often engage in plural activities: We are on the phone, reading something on our desk, and also attending to someone who just came in. And we are attempting to give our best to each of these three situations! Plural activities split us, stress us, and accelerate us even higher.

How much of your stress is a consequence of your fast pace? By accurately self-monitoring, you can assess your own total reaction. You may then decide to slow down in order to achieve the following:

1. To increase the quality of your performance.
2. To enjoy your experience more fully.
3. To enable others to enjoy you more.
4. To increase your productivity.
5. To decrease your stress level.
6. Possibly to live longer and last longer.

Take a moment and think about your own work situation with its particular responsibilities and job tasks. Check out each of the above reasons in turn.

1. By slowing down, how might the quality of your work become better? How will slowing down affect the tasks you perform, the way you relate to people, the reports you write, and all the rest? If we take time to study a situation or a problem, we may end up doing a better job. Would

certain decisions be better ones if you took the time to think, to plan, to get all the background data, and to consider various possibilities? I am not advising procrastination here, but a real increase in quality.

2. By slowing down and experiencing each moment fully, we typically feel more enjoyment in our experience. All our senses come alive. We listen more carefully and see more thoroughly; our senses of smell and touch and taste enrich and sharpen. This becomes quite apparent in a simple daily experience like eating. Try it. Before you eat, first look at your food. Verbalize to yourself (or to someone else) what you see. Then and only then, smell it. Allow the associations and nostalgia to flow. Stop for a moment and enjoy them. Then listen to your food (some food really does make sounds—give it a try). Then taste it slowly, moving the food gently around your mouth, seeking out different taste sensations on different parts of your tongue. How much more enjoyable does your eating experience become?

3. If you decide to experience the people around you slowly, you will probably take more time to relate to them. You will take time to listen to them. You may well find that you enjoy them and your work more. Consider how much more your secretary or spouse or coworker might enjoy being around you if you slow down in relating to them.

4. Why would productivity actually increase by slowing down? Ridiculous, you say? You could be right, but consider these possibilities: In some job tasks, a slower pace means fewer mistakes and less time needed to re-do. Often, taking the time in the beginning means getting all the facts, hearing the instructions carefully, and truly understanding what is being asked and what is being said. Thinking through a problem beforehand under slower, creative, less stressful conditions can result in decisions that cause fewer future problems. This also increases our productivity. When a supervisor/manager takes more time with subordinates, it can pay off in higher morale and more cooperation

from subordinates. People feel less like they are being is-
sued commands or that the manager is merely cracking the
whip. Take the time to give instructions. Be sure that your
subordinate truly understands what needs to be done. Subordinates feel less tense when the manager slows down, and
they actually work better! The owner of a large plant nursery learned this the hard way. His own style was fast, restless, and hurrying. His nursery supervisor was a slower,
calmer person. When the hectic boss quickly expressed a
demand or a concern, the supervisor didn't jump fast
enough. The boss felt that the man just wasn't with it. The
boss fired him. He then got a new supervisor who jumped
every time he jumped. The new man was fast and hurried.
The boss, however, got only the appearance of action. He
reported, "Things fell apart, and productivity lowered. I
wished I had the old supervisor back. He really got things
done."

5. When your stress level lowers to more moderate levels, we have clearly noted that you will bump into people
less while hurrying down the hall and that you will reduce
wasteful activity, worry, and spinning of wheels. Your positive qualities are more likely to emerge. You will consider
and be considerate; you will use the depth of your intelligence, experience, and so on.

6. Whether you will live longer is debatable. Some of
you may well say, "Do you call that living?" or, "It's boring
and uninteresting." Actually, it may be different for some of
you, but it will not be boring. It will mean a new style—not
passivity but activity—at a different pace. Some readers
will have to experience this in order to appreciate it. The
slower style is exciting and enjoyable, but it is clearly different.

How do you proceed to make the change? How do you
slow down if you are the hurried type? Try any of the following:

1. First and foremost, buy the concept. Or at least be
willing to give it a try. Say to yourself, rushing = waste of

time; rushing = too high stress; rushing = behavior I am ashamed of, and so on. Or say, slower (and quiet) people can be effective and highly productive. Accept the idea, at least long enough to give it a try.

2. Choose an activity that you currently speed up in—for example, driving, eating, impatience in lines, giving instructions, reading time cards, or dictating letters—and deliberately slow it down. Try to seek in the experience something enjoyable, fascinating, and interesting. Deliberately turn the negative into a positive. Use waiting to think, to talk to strangers, or to read that book you carry in your pocket or purse. Take control of the situation and turn it into something enjoyable to you—a new experience of enjoyment.

3. Accept the idea that plural activities (except for strict routine) are time wasting, uncreative, and possibly dangerous (too much plurality while driving a car or while listening to an important customer can lead to trouble). Concentrate solely on one activity at a time. Give yourself fully, without distraction. Give your best—your total self. Notice the quality/quantity of the results.

4. When relevant, say to yourself, "What counts is not if I get there first, but if I get there at all"; "It's not whether I win or lose, but whether I enjoy what I'm doing"; "Not speed, but distance."

5. Deliberately seek out certain quiet activities and make the conscious effort to find enjoyment in them. For example, spend some time watching the waves or the sunset; listen to a brook or a symphony (not while reading or doing anything else); go for a walk with a year-and-a-half-old, holding the child's hand. Make up your own list.

6. Try a ten-minute mini-slow at work. If you expect a particularly stressful situation coming up, take ten minutes before you face that situation and spend the time doing one of the following:

Taking a few minutes to look out the window in order to gain a different perspective.

Go for a short vigorous walk (if you are tense) or a quiet aimless one (avoid thinking while walking; afterwards reflect).

Do a relaxation/stretch/breathing or other exercise (take the full ten minutes).

Think about the other person's point of view, seek it out, understand it, even attempt to savor it (why shouldn't he or she have a point of view?).

Read over the Recall Reminder List that you are filling out at the back of this book.

When you face that anticipated situation, take the time to listen rather than to tell.

Slowdowns do not always work. They might not increase productivity; they might, as some of you fear, decrease your work output. You might find it too tense and stressful for you to change your pace to a slower one. You might find the trade-offs unfavorable or intolerable. Nothing in this chapter is to be construed as supporting evasiveness, indecision, or the inability to face responsibilities. The purpose of slowing down is to make you a better employee. Will it work for you? You'll never really know until you try.

RECALL REMINDER

SLOW DOWN

You might want to experiment with slowing down to see what values it might have for you.

1. I would like to try slowing down while doing

_____and see if it might increase the quality of my work.

2. I would like to slow down while doing

_____and test out whether it increases my productivity.

3. If I slowed down doing_____, might it result in more enjoyment for me or for people around me?

4. I would like to slow down doing

_____and see if it lowers my stress to more reasonable and rational levels.

11
CRISES AND EMERGENCIES

George is a bank supervisor. His tellers, clerks, and others see him as the primary source of help, assistance with problems, and knowledge of company rules. He also deals with complaints from customers. He also tries, every day, to monitor what's going on in several departments. Often, one or two people are waiting for him with their problems, complaints, and dissatisfactions. He may be working with some important paper problems at his desk, be interrupted for an urgent telephone call, or have a subordinate hovering over him with still another problem. When he has a chance to stop, he often feels confused, almost overwhelmed. By the end of the day, George is shot, emotionally exhausted. He's putting out brush fires all day long. He's available for interruption at any time. Anyone can get to him, and they often do. He's managing his job by a style often called management by crisis.

Perhaps, like George, you find your work day plagued with interruptions. People seek you out for a variety of reasons, all of which are extremely important to them:

They depend on you for answers.

They come to you regularly for help.
They come with problems to be solved.
You have special knowledge or skills.
You are the strong and able one.
You deal with complaints or discipline
    problems.
People come to you with high emotion
    and they want action now.
People come with complaints or anger.

Whatever your job title, you may find that you have gotten into this style of managing your job. It is not necessary that your job be graced with the title "manager" for you to adopt this style. You may be a secretary, a school principal, the vice principal in a high school, a trouble-shooter, a computer specialist, a repair person, a doctor, or a mother with demanding children. Your personality style can keep you hopping all the time. You're hopping because you are the center, the focus, the problem solver, the answer giver, or the necessary individual sought out by others. Others call on you any time, and you respond—just like Pavlov's dogs. Someone rings your bell, and you salivate. And some people get awfully wet feet (from all that salivating—see Figure 11–1) by the end of the day. It's a hectic style of operating—all those external stressors coming at you.

Whatever your job title (or lack of it), you may decide to get out of this style of managing your work. You may want to do this for any one of the following reasons:

You can be interrupted at any time, and this wrecks
    havoc with your own productivity.
People typically come to you with high emotion, and
    coping with their emotions raises your own.
You may find it difficult and time consuming to get
    back to your own work after each interruption.
Typically, you don't have time/energy/strength left to
    deal with the basic functions of your job or with
    what *you* consider important.
Your stress level rises to objectionable levels.

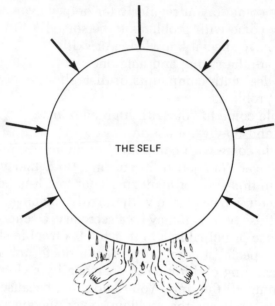

The Wet Feet Syndrome
Figure 11–1

If you've made the decision to reduce or eliminate this style, two general approaches have been found effective.

SCHEDULING CRISES AND EMERGENCIES
The first approach is to schedule all these crises and emergencies for a certain hour or two during the day instead of having them come at you all day long. Typically, this is done by informing your stressors that you are available to help them any time between, say, eleven to twelve A.M. or three to four P.M., but not at any other time. What happens to most of those crises and emergencies that absolutely need you? Many people who try this discover that most of the problems get solved without them. These urgent, pressing crises get taken care of, and only a small number actually reach you during that eleven to twelve or three to four hour.

Not everybody is comfortable or feels able to schedule

their problems and crises. Think for a moment how this could possibly be modified for your own particular job situation. Perhaps you cannot schedule all of your external stressors, but you can schedule some of them. You can comfortably ask some people to restrict their interruptions; you could not ask others to do this.

Many people feel that the Big Boss is one external stressor that you can not schedule. Whenever he calls, you want to jump! It might, however, be worthwhile talking this over with your immediate boss (if not the big one) and finding out what he or she considers to be crucial. In one organization, a Big Boss was asked if he always wanted his subordinates to stop what they were doing when he called. He thought about this a moment and said, "Not if you are with a customer; that customer comes first." Check it out. You may be surprised!

Another way to modify the scheduling approach is to reverse it by scheduling at least some time without interruptions and then letting all those crises and problems come in the rest of the day. Schedule, say, between nine and ten in the morning, for work without interruption. All the rest of the day may remain as it is now. Again, most of the problems can wait until after ten o'clock or get solved on their own. You don't get as much unstressed time this way, but it may fit more comfortably into some work situations. One organization I heard of set the first hour of each day to have the switchboard cut off, no conferences, and no visiting. Everyone had a full hour every day of uninterrupted work time. Consider how much work people could get done during that solitary hour. How would that work for you?

PRIORITIZE AND DELEGATE

The second approach is a bit more complicated, but it usually satisfies any of the above objections we might have to scheduling other people. This approach is accomplished in several steps.

Step One—*Prioritize.* List all those crises, problems, and emergencies. In consultation and discussion with other relevant persons at work (such as secretaries, subordinates, or the immediate boss), list all the crises that have occurred in the past and all the ones that you can anticipate in the future. Then sit down by yourself and prioritize that list in terms of which ones you feel you must deal with. Let's say that you and your consultors come up with fifty crises. You prioritize and will probably come up with only a small number of that fifty that you feel you must deal with. You may have trouble believing that, but make that list of past crises in the cool calm of day, and most of the urgency will be gone. Even in the medical field, there are only a handful of actual medical emergencies. Remember now that we are basing the decision not on the emotion of the person coming to you but on your best decision (as a specialist in your job, as a professional, or as a lifetime career person). What do you feel you must deal with? Out of the fifty, you will probably end up with about a half a dozen that, to you, are true emergencies.

Step two—*Screening.* Then the remaining forty-four (out of the total fifty) must be separated from the six that you must deal with. That requires a screening process. Someone in your work situation often has a position where they do this screening (secretary, receptionist, or assistant). If not, in some cases a simple written form can be developed to be filled in. This screening person, and it is hoped that there is such a person available, must be selected carefully for this position and must be trained for this screening work. The selection should be based on a simple Vocational Placement Formula. This formula is calculated to reduce job stress. The formula is as follows:

Competence = Enjoy (Vocational Placement Formula)

The formula simply says, "That which we enjoy doing best, we do the most competently." And that which we do the most competently, we enjoy doing. Don't select a screening person who must deal with complaining, angry, dissatisfied, or needful people unless that screening person truly enjoys dealing with high emotion in others. The person who wants to get to you with the problem, complaint, or crisis is typically experiencing high emotion. They want something, they usually want it right now, and they want it from you. All that emotion must be dealt with. The Vocational Placement Formula says that some secretaries, receptionists, and assistants enjoy (are more competent) writing words or typing words or reports; some are competent with numbers, charts, and figures; others are competent in (enjoy) dealing with people who are upset. Select the right person. If necessary, train him or her.*

Wouldn't it be neat if everyone was placed in a job based solely on the above formula? If the person who fixes your car, helps you with your bad back, or cooks and serves your food truly enjoys what he or she is doing, you could then expect high quality and competent performance. What a neat way to go!

The last step in managing these crises and emergencies is to arrange for the handling of the other forty-four situations identified by your screening person. Some of these situations are automatically dealt with at that point, because the high emotion is dissipated. They can wait, or they get solved on their own. Others need to be delegated or referred elsewhere. If there are persons available to whom you can delegate, these should also be specialists chosen not just for their knowledge but for their skill in dealing with high emotion in others. If you have no subordinates, you generally refer the crises and emergencies to other individuals. Some people get to be quite skilled at doing this. In a work situation, we don't want, however, to just dump those forty-four; we want to make sure that the person with high

---

* See Chapter 8 on the Do-nut and Chapter 9 on venting for techniques in dealing with high emotion in others. Train your screening person in using these techniques.

emotion feels that you *care.* This is a vital part of what the screening person does in handling the high emotion. Remember the last time you called the doctor when you were in a state of high emotion? Was it possibly the pediatrician? You were concerned and afraid; possibly you anticipated rejection and felt angry. Just talking to someone who seems to care about your problem or who seems to understand it goes a long way to reducing your high need to "talk to the doctor." Obviously, there are some situations where you should get to the doctor, and a good medical staff screens out those true medical emergencies and gets you to the doctor fast.

Another technique that is sometimes of help in dealing with crises and emergencies is called the "Five-Year Rule." This simple little rule is an aid in giving us perspective. During emotionally charged situations, we desperately need to look at things in terms of a broader point of view than the narrow, constricted one we feel at the height of emotion. Sometimes, even a few hours later the crisis has lost its emergency nature, and we can look back on it quite differently. Certainly five years hence most situations can be looked at quite calmly, with little or no stress. The Five-Year Rule offers you the perspective of five years in the future. Five years from now, as you look back on this crucial emergency, how important will it seem then? Many of the stressful problems we face today lose a good deal of their emotion under the scrutiny of this rule. Applying it can, at times, give us the perspective to be more rational and more reasonable.

There are, of course, some present-day issues that truly have significant effects five years from now. What are they in your work and in your life? Many individuals, when they consider this question, come up with basic significant issues in their life: their families, their own personal health, their relationships to people on the job, their financial security, their long-range professional goals, perhaps their capital projects. Generally, there are not too many day-to-day issues that are truly significant.

Try adapting some of these processes to your job or even to your family situation. Schedule, screen, or combine these in order to restrict that daily barrage from the outside world. Or try the Five-Year Rule. Remember, if you salivate too often when that bell rings, your feet will be mighty wet.

RECALL REMINDER

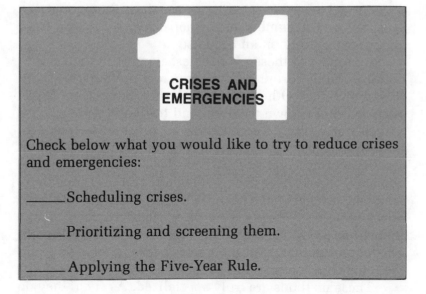

CRISES AND EMERGENCIES

Check below what you would like to try to reduce crises and emergencies:

_____Scheduling crises.

_____Prioritizing and screening them.

_____ Applying the Five-Year Rule.

MUSCLE RELAXATION METHODS

If you've longed to relax and unwind and have found it difficult to do so, one of the methods described in this chapter may be for you. Man's longing for a state of calmness and repose has probably been an eternal one. In his search for ways to achieve this condition, man has, throughout the ages, evolved a number of methods. Many of these have deep roots in religion and philosophy.

A number of these approaches, along with their ties to religion and philosophy, have taken root in Western society in recent times. Other approaches, too, have been developed within our own tradition and technology.

In our efforts to reduce the anxiousness of our age, these approaches have fortunately been given a great deal of attention. Consequently, they have developed considerably. Numerous books have been written describing each of these methods, teachers have been trained in them, schools have developed, and courses have been made available. Large followings of individuals have found in each of these methods helpful guidance in their search for that elusive calmness, that inner peace that many of us long for.

These methods are truly specialized. As such, they do

require specific training led by a teacher who is a specialist. You may find the reading material on each method helpful, but in almost all cases, the books recommend the use of a teacher. A teacher is considered necessary not only to learn the specifics of the method initially but especially in order to maintain regular practice. And in general, regular practice in these methods is required before you have become adept enough in the method to find it useful.

Fortunately, individual workshops, classes, and full courses in most of these methods are generally quite available. Places that offer adult classes, such as "Y's" and adult education schools, offer some of these methods. But also available are the specialized teachers and schools that privately offer such training. Since these schools seek out students, they publicize widely: By watching newspapers, bulletin boards, and organizational newsletters and by using telephone directories or inquiring about classes, you should, in most reasonably large communities, be able to get specialized training in any of these methods. If that fails, you can give self-teaching a try. Your public library or bookstore should have at least some of the books written about each method.

Each of the methods will be briefly described here, and your appetite may be whetted to pursue training in the method of your choice. The specialized muscle relaxation techniques are the following:

PROGRESSIVE RELAXATION (developed by Jacobson in the early 1900s).

YOGA (Eastern, eternal, even available on TV).

MASSAGE (respectable and traditional).

BIOFEEDBACK (new; requires equipment).

MEDITATION techniques (typically religious, now for everyone).

SELF-HYPNOSIS (and other approaches involving fantasy or imagery).

Let's consider each in turn.

PROGRESSIVE RELAXATION

Edmund Jacobson's (1970) method of progressively relaxing each of your muscle groups is probably known to many of us in one form or another. This approach is based on the theory that if you relax those muscles that have accumulated emotional tension, then your mind (emotions) also relaxes. Jacobson's studies stem from the beginning of the century. He used instruments that he developed in conjunction with the Bell Telephone Company to show that when we try to relax our bodies in the usual ways (by sitting, lying down, etc.), we do not relax completely. The method he devised to achieve this more complete relaxation is called "Progressive Relaxation." In a popular form that many of us are familiar with, one lies on one's back and starts first relaxing one's toes, then the foot, leg, and so on until the muscle groups in the entire body are relaxed. Relaxation is not an effort in itself, but simply the absence of effort.

The process of learning to do this may come quickly or may be lengthy. The method has been used successfully with a wide variety of individuals and situations. I have heard of individuals achieving relaxation in situations ranging from men awaiting combat during World War II to patients trying to gain rest in hospital beds. One man reported to me that he used it to learn to sleep in the tight, tense, noisy quarters of a submarine. You might find this method helpful after the day's work, during lunch hour, or before going to sleep. After you learn Progressive Relaxation lying down, you can usually achieve the same muscle relaxation in a sitting position. In spite of Jacobson's recommendations for lengthy training, many individuals learn by themselves and fairly quickly. Although obviously everyone might not find it so, it does seem to be one of the easier methods to learn. Progressive Relaxation is sometimes taught in courses labeled "Stress Reduction" that are available at YMCAs and YWCAs, through adult education courses, and in similar places. Check these out if you are interested.

YOGA—AND BREATHING TECHNIQUES

Yoga has become so popular that it probably requires little introduction here. As a means of achieving relaxation, it, too, is based on the use of muscles (and breathing) in order to achieve mental or emotional relaxation. It has other values, as well, in affecting body flexibility, because of the stretching nature of the various Yoga positions. Yoga often involves a warm-up set of physical exercises that, as a minimum, involve the large muscles. This in itself provides some of the stress release described in this book as LMA. Yoga is also related to meditation, and Yoga teachers often see meditation as part of the entire Yoga approach.

I'm particularly impressed with the way properly done Yoga exercises force the individual to breathe in a way that produces relaxation. Breathing in itself is a form of relaxation ("Before you say anything, take a deep breath"). The methods of prepared childbirth (for example, LaMaze) teach the expectant mother specific breathing exercises as a form of muscle relaxation. This controlled breathing can actually reduce the pain experienced during labor and childbirth.

Yoga, too, is generally not a difficult technique for many individuals. Since there are many different bodily positions in Yoga, some positions are easy for some bodies, although difficult for others. It just depends on your body. Courses are extensively available, and even public TV (your local PBS station) provides a regular teaching program. This is another easy one to give a try.

MASSAGE

Massage has been a traditionally effective means for directly relieving that tension we have accumulated in our muscles. You've probably had someone squeeze your shoulders or massage your upper back and have felt the release of tension that results from this simple, informal massage. Usually, our emotional reaction is, "That feels good". Emotional satisfaction inevitably accompanies the release of muscle tension. Massage, like other muscle techniques, is based on the same principle of emotion (stress) becoming buried (embedded) in our muscles. In massage, the muscles are directly (physically) dealt with rather than dealing with them indirectly through some mental form or meditation. Direct manipulation of those tense muscles can relax the tight, contracted, "knotty" areas. And as this occurs, the buried emotion is released. Often during massage, particularly intense massage, many deeply embedded emotions— even some from childhood—are released as the muscles are freed of their emotional burden.

Massage also has the value of human touch (see Chapter 13, Pleasurable Goodies). Someone cares about us and is communicating this physically. Possibly this returns us to some earlier, infant-like, being cared for state. This human communication can considerably enhance the muscle release value of massage.

Massage has its own schools and specialists. Traditional, Swedish and other European forms of massage have been supplemented by newer methods. One of the more well known is Rolfing, named after Dr. Ida Rolf, a former biochemist. This form of massage is a form of body restructuring (sometimes the term *body work* is used to describe a form of massage) that requires deep, heavy pressure. Rolfing often frees up deeply embedded emotions and therefore is sometimes used as an adjunct to psychotherapy.

Massage does require the services of another person, although limited self-massage is possible. Finding that specialist may be something of a problem because of the tawdry reputation of massage parlors. Many communities require licensing of masseurs, and schools are available that pro-

vide the necessary training to meet the licensing requirement. Probably the most comfortable way to seek out someone who does massage is through some organization or
institution, such as a growth center, holistic health center,
or religious retreat. There are not many books available, but
one of them is especially practical (Downing, 1972). It is
used as a text in training courses, but it should also be helpful to the general reader.

BIOFEEDBACK

Of the techniques in this chapter, biofeedback is the newest
and probably the most exciting. It is typically American in
its approach, being based on both electronic technology and
on the principle of gaining conscious control over oneself.
Although biofeedback lacks the philosophical and spiritual
heritage of other approaches, the basic ideas underlying it
are not new. What is new—or at least new to medical
science—is the concept of gaining conscious control over
physiological processes that for some time were considered
to be involuntary. Through biofeedback training, an individual can learn to control such physiological processes as
heartbeat, blood pressure, muscle tension, constriction and
contraction of blood vessels, skin temperature, and brain
waves. Up until the advent of biofeedback, most of these
physiological processes were thought to be mainly or completely out of conscious control.*

In biofeedback, this conscious control is achieved
through the use of an electronic feedback device that is
hooked up to measure continuously whatever process one
is trying to control. In muscle control, for example, the electronic sensor is attached to a muscle, and the data from that
muscle is amplified and fed into a read-out device (this can

---

* Except for a few rare individuals, such as yogis or fakirs, who were able
to demonstrate some conscious control over heartbeat, skin temperature,
and so on.

be a needle, a light, or a sound). By receiving this continuous visual or auditory feedback, the subject is able to continuously monitor whether his or her conscious control is having the desired effect. With the aid of this electronic monitoring, the subject gets instant feedback on the success of his or her efforts to change the physiological measure. With proper training, he or she is able to make the desired change.

What kind of physical changes that affect stress are controllable? Primarily, of course, the muscles. As with LMA and the other methods in this chapter, tension in the muscles can be reduced for general stress release. With a biofeedback device for measuring and reading out muscle tension and with proper training, muscle tension can be relieved. A great deal of research has been done in testing the value of biofeedback technique in accomplishing this. Results have been encouraging (see Brown, 1977). Often, biofeedback has been used in conjunction with other relaxation techniques (Meditation, Yoga, or Progressive Relaxation).

This is an approach with a great deal of scientific interest, using methods that are readily measurable and testable. There should be continued expansion of biofeedback services to assist individuals with a variety of problems, including, of course, stress. These services are generally obtained through medical or psychiatric clinics and occasionally through licensed psychologists. Although some biofeedback equipment can be purchased for as little as one hundred dollars, this is obviously not an approach you should try on your own. Seek professional help.

MEDITATION

The previous relaxation techniques in this chapter are primarily muscle oriented. Those techniques base their stress reduction value on relieving tension in the muscles or body. Meditation differs only in that its approach, on first glance, seems more mental. The emphasis is on achieving a highly special state of mind.

Because of the oneness of mind and body, achieving this mental state *can* be effective in producing changes in the body. Research on meditation has verified that the meditation process can do just that. Although the interpretation of this data is controversial (see Brown, 1977), studies have shown measurable physical changes in the body resulting from meditation (Wallace, 1972; Benson, 1975).

Meditation is a term used to describe any number of different spiritual or mental approaches to achieving a special state of mind or consciousness. Many of these approaches are highly religious and philosophical in their tradition. The religious traditions of meditation are not solely Eastern in their history. One author describes at least twelve different approaches to meditation, covering the world's major religions—forms of Christianity, Judaism, Hinduism, Buddhism, and .so on (Goleman, 1977). Even the Quakers have written about a form of meditation that has value in the worship experience for members of the Society of Friends (Crom, 1974).

Because there are so many different approaches, there are many applications, with differing effects. Sometimes meditation is used to refer to a concentrated thought process; for example, meditate on a specific subject, such as "love." The terms used to describe this process may be thoughtful, reflective, or intellectual. In many of the approaches to meditation, a quite different attitude is required. The terms frequently used are the following: passive, increased awareness, insight, and watchfulness. This is not a conscious thinking process, nor is it a problem-solving process. Numerous authors offer special guidance in achieving this state (see, for example, LeShan, 1974; Benson, 1975; Maharishi Mahesh Yogi, 1968).

Even though meditation is approached through a mental process, many authors recognize that stress accumulates in the muscles and therefore recommend a relaxed physical state before beginning to meditate. Some, in fact, specifically suggest using Jacobson's Progressive Relaxation as a prelude to the meditation technique.

Meditation, of all the techniques in this chapter, is probably one of the more difficult to apply. It may well require extensive training, persistence, and the guidance of a helpful teacher. Probably fewer people are able to achieve its maximum effects (see Glasser, 1976) than to see the effects of other approaches. There is, however, value in taking the time once or twice a day just to be by oneself in a quiet state (see Chapters 18 and 17 on Me-Act and Solitude). Research has shown that some of the same physiological changes produced by meditation can be produced by a restful state (Brown, 1977). Shorn of all its religious, spiritual, and philosophical bases, this quiet state alone is significant in stress reduction. If you are able, in addition, to gain religious or spiritual meaning in this meditative experience, you can enhance its value for you even further.

There is much reading available on meditation. Courses are generally available, too. In seeking a teacher, Lawrence LeShan, in his book *How to Meditate* (1974), suggests the following considerations:

> *What kind of person is the teacher?. . .Look at the teacher and see what his approach and work have done for* him. *What are his human relationships? If he implies you should simply follow directions without asking why, but trust him, he is on a guru trip. If he tells you he is imparting "secret" knowledge reserved for special people (like you) and that you must swear never to reveal it to the uninitiated, I advise seeking the nearest exit immediately. . .If he promises you meditation training, inner growth and development and then organizes the process as big business. . .this is opposite to every known reasonable principle in the field.*

SELF HYPNOSIS

Hypnosis has traditionally had extensive use as a technique in medicine. Freud, you may recall, used hypnosis in his early days as a step in the development of later psychoanalytic methods. Hypnosis today is used in certain medical, dental, and psychiatric situations. A number of the specialists who use it also recommend its use as a self-help. The term *self-hypnosis* is used, as are other terms, such as Autogenic Training.

Hypnosis is based on the concept of suggestion. The power of suggestion in influencing our behavior is clearly evident. The powerful placebo effect and other similar influences are probably primarily due to the suggestibility in all of us. Self-hypnosis is a tool that enables you to choose whatever specific suggestions you want to become important in your life. Suggestions can be chosen to relax, to induce sleep, or to reduce smoking and other unwanted habits. For stress reduction, hypnosis attempts to indirectly influence both body (muscle) and mind through suggestion. Different teachers (authors) offer different techniques for inducing hypnosis and for using these suggestions.

Hypnosis is an approach that may seem far out for some of us. Authors and instructors sometimes make extensive claims for self-hypnosis. There is no question, however, that self-hypnosis has been used by some individuals as a valuable tool for achieving certain changes (goals) in their lives. It can be used to achieve relaxation or used in conjunction with other methods.

It may be more difficult to find courses and specialized training in self-hypnosis than in the other methods described in this chapter. If you are interested, as a starter, you can read some of the references. Perhaps these will enable you to give it a try on your own.

Related to self-hypnosis and sometimes part of it (Bernhardt & Martin, 1977) are methods that use imagination and imagery to help us move into a more relaxed, peaceful state. These techniques rely heavily on our abilities to fantasize.

We can influence our fantasies (control them, if you wish) and propel them roughly where we want them to go. Imagine, dream, and fantasize, about peace and calmness, and you are well on the way to achieving that kind of emotional state.

One typical approach to this asks you to choose a scene that is a very peaceful one for you. You may choose a sandy beach, an idyllic rural scene, or whatever represents your calm dream. It is often easier to achieve this fantasy if you are in a relaxed state, eyes closed, perhaps lying down in a darkened room. It also often helps to listen to a soothing voice or calming music. All this helps to set the mood for you. If you try this alone, try a tape recorder with the taped voice telling you to relax, to fantasize your scene, and to put yourself into it. Use music if it helps. Add whatever other relaxing suggestions you want to recall at that point. You can adapt this considerably to your own interests and credibility. Different imagery approaches use different fantasies and different ways to set the mood. Some of this approach, too, comes close to some of the meditation techniques in the way you achieve the relaxed state.

You can try relaxed imagery on your own or with the help of an instructor. Some individuals find it relatively easy, even fun. This is still another way to get your body/mind to reverse its tenseness. It just might work for you.

RECALL REMINDER

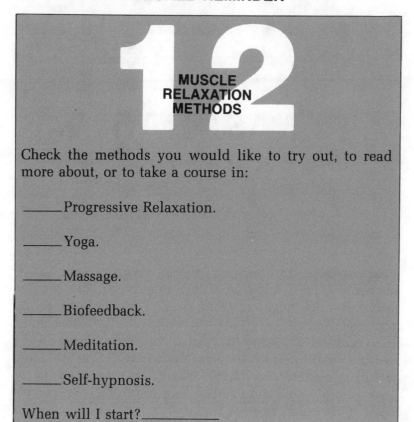

MUSCLE RELAXATION METHODS

Check the methods you would like to try out, to read more about, or to take a course in:

_____Progressive Relaxation.

_____Yoga.

_____Massage.

_____Biofeedback.

_____Meditation.

_____Self-hypnosis.

When will I start?_____

PLEASURABLE GOODIES

There are a host of personal pleasures that we enjoy, that change our pace, and that relieve our stress. They may, in addition, release us and comfort us. These are indeed our personal "therapies." They do us good. They feel good.

They are also good in a true moral sense. These are the healthy goodies. They do us no harm (not like certain other goodies, unmentioned here, but to be discussed later). These are positive and healthy; they are right, even proper. What more could one ask for?

There are a wide assortment of such goodies. The list below is offered merely to aid you in recognizing the full range of alternatives available. Perhaps, too, by perusing this list you will recall past pleasures that you've more recently given up in your life. Perhaps you've denied yourself those goodies because of the heavy press of work and responsibility. This may be the time to dig them out again! Here's a list to get you thinking:

MUSIC (listening to it; singing or playing it).
LAUGHTER (but not the hostile kind).
POETRY, sayings, and slogans.

PRAYER (and other religious comfort).
APOLOGIZING (and avoiding a great deal of stress).
HUGGING (and other forms of touch).
CRYING (perhaps not so pleasant, but a good release).
RITUALS AND TRADITIONS (family, religious, or social ones).
SPENDING MONEY (if you enjoy doing it).
PLAYING (with or without toys).
HOT BATHS AND HOT TUBS (saunas, turkish baths, etc.).
REST (sleep, cat naps, doing nothing).

Let's take a brief look at the way people use these goodies for relief or release of stress.

MUSIC

Many people recognize the value of music in their lives—the pleasures of listening, the joy of singing, and the satisfaction of playing. All of us are capable of listening, and the only requirement seems to be that the music is of our own choice. Listening to unwanted music is noise, and noise, as we have seen, adds to our stress level. Listening to music totally, not using it as background for reading or other activities, can be emotionally consuming. It can transport and envelop us. It can remove us emotionally and mentally from our usual state. It can also relax us physically.

Singing can be a real release and an opportunity to express feelings. Singing can change our moods from gloomy and unsatisfied states to more pleasant, happy ones. Singing can provide some muscle release (particularly if done with great vigor). I sometimes use singing this way. Occasionally, after a stressful day, I find that I have a long drive in the car ahead of me. I am pushed for time and must get to the driving. I would prefer, if I had the choice, to engage in LMA—to swim, bike, or walk. I solve this dilemma by singing while driving. I sing anything that comes to my mind. I sing loudly, lustily, and probably not too well

(I never listen). It helps a great deal to release my stress while my body feels trapped behind the wheel. The quality of the singing is unimportant.

Playing music is another release that can be powerful. Some people play regularly—as often as once a day—and consider it highly therapeutic. Others play (piano, organ, guitar, etc.) more rarely but do so when the need arises. They may then play for several hours. If you are skilled at playing a musical instrument, you have probably already found out just how it works for you in dealing with stress.

If you feel that you can't sing or play, you can, of course, learn. Learning something new like this does take time and some long-term discipline (see Chapters 22 and 23). But music in one form or another does remain a viable option for almost all of us.

LAUGHTER AND HUMOR

We've all been in situations where a joke told at the right moment in a tense situation relieved a great deal of stress. This use of humor is spontaneous. Whether we could plan to use such humor in our next stress situation is highly doubtful. And yet we can recognize the value of humor. It has often been pointed out that laughing, and particularly a humorous view of life, seems to take away some of the pain. Seeing the humor in our difficulties or in our pain requires a state of distancing. This emotional distancing alone can obviously be of help in lowering our level of stress. We often joke when we feel uncomfortable. The friendly response of others provides a shared warmth that takes away some of the discomfort. Humor has also recently been emphasized as a possible source of healing (Moody, 1978). Many of us have heard of Norman Cousins, the *Saturday Review* editor, who used humor as the basic method in curing a serious and painful illness (Cousins, 1977).

Some researchers have tested the value of a specially designed "humor environment." This environment had fun apparatus, cartoons, jokes, silly dress-up clothes, and the like. The researchers were able to measure actual positive changes in people's emotions before and after spending time in such an environment (see Moody, 1978). As yet, I haven't recommended setting up such a "humor room" in offices and factories (although I have suggested other kinds of rooms). How would you like to have one right on your floor, down the hall, maybe next to the elevator? Try asking for that one at the next negotiating time. At the very least, you should get a laugh!

The kind of humor that seems most stress releasing is the kind where we are capable of laughing at ourselves. We make fun of our own traits, laugh at our habits, or joke about our weaknesses. This is one way where humor can come awfully close to crying. Life seems awfully painful—so ridiculous and so hopeless that we burst out laughing. We say, "How stupid" or "What a joke I am"—but in a warm, accepting tone, devoid of any self-criticism or recrimination. This is obviously a far cry from the humor that makes fun of or ridicules someone. The name for that is hostility (see Chapter 3).

You might deliberately try to behave more humorously. Sometimes you might be able to pull it off. I don't know what the right conditions are to make it work, but I do know that sometimes it does work. "Laugh and the whole world laughs with you" recognizes the value of a humorous attitude. Cultivate and encourage it. Observe its effect on your stress leveling.

POETRY

Poets and other talented writers have been able to tune in to the human condition and put it down in words. They do this in ways that serve as comfort and reassurance to many of us. Almost all of us have our favored poems or writers. Some of us have briefer sayings, phrases, or even slogans that help us in times of stress. Some people carry these written words about in their wallets or purses, others in their minds. Some post them on walls or frame them for all to see. Sources range from the classical (Shakespeare), religious (Bible, psalms, Talmud, Confucius, etc.), to the ridiculous (Ogden Nash, the comics, joke books, cartoons, etc.). Typical examples are: "Today is the first day of the rest of your life," "Take one thing at a time," or "Go placidly amid the noise and haste. . . ." (*Desiderata*). Reading these during times of stress can be comforting, reassuring, or uplifting.

PRAYER AND WORSHIP

Praying, for some of us, offers us a time of calmness or meditation, a time of comfort or healing. Some people use prayer as the opportunity to reach out to someone who cares, to someone who always listens, understands, and loves. This provides an opportunity similar in some respects to the venting experience described in Chapter 9. Religion in all its forms helps us to deal with the ultimate stresses of birth and death and with many of the crises in between. Whatever the nature of your own spirituality, it can be a source of help and comfort in times of high stress. I can gain a tranquil feeling of peace just by entering a large, old church and quietly resting there for just a few minutes. Weekly attendance at church or synagogue can be a time of inspiration and comfort. It can provide, too, some of the unchanging values of tradition as well as a regular source of social support. If religion is in an upsurge right now in our society, possibly it is partially because of the help religion can offer us in times of stress. Reach out for this spirituality or regain some of the values you may have had earlier in your life.

APOLOGIES

Apologizing can be a powerful means of avoiding a fair amount of stress. It can serve this purpose because there are times when we all behave in ways that we disapprove of. I sometimes feel uncomfortable admitting this, but it is true. Typically, this behavior occurs when we are already stressed, high on our emotional temperature graph. We might, for example, do the following:

Say things we shouldn't have said.
Behave badly toward someone.
Act unreasonable or irrational.
Flash out in anger.
Perform poorly at work.
Deal with a situation inefficiently.

Whatever the behavior is, we often find ourselves, after the situation occurs, having to face the consequences of our behavior. Sometimes we are criticized or attacked. At this point, we add to our stress level considerably by attempting to defend that behavior of ours. We may find it difficult to defend behavior that is indefensible, but we do it anyway! This can get us into higher emotion—exaggeration, even lying. Especially, it causes us to defend by attack. Whatever kind of stressful shenanigans we drag ourselves into, all this can be clearly avoided by the simple act of apology. "I'm sorry, that's not the way I want to behave," or "I really disapprove of doing that; I'm sorry I did it." At the very least, this disarms your potential attacker and saves you from having to face the brunt of his or her emotion.

It is sometimes pointed out that apologies cannot be overdone. If, however, you are apologizing a great deal for your behavior, you'd better start making some changes. If you apologize too frequently to your boss, he or she may decide that your unreasonable, irrational behavior is not that infrequent but is probably your typical mode of behavior. Make some changes by considering the need to lower your emotions to more reasonable levels (use any of the techniques in this part of the book). Or, if appropriate, consider using the Do-nut to lower your negative behavior.

Your apologies must obviously be sincere. They cannot be used as a technique only, as a gimmick. You must truly disapprove of behaving badly. You will probably feel the need to make amends for your bad behavior in order to correct the consequences.

Sometimes people are uncomfortable about making apologies. They admit to a "Superman" or "Superwoman" myth. If you always have to be right and don't like getting caught in the wrong, you are obviously setting yourself up for a heavy stress load. To err is a most human trait. Give apology a try. It becomes easier with practice.

HUGGING AND OTHER FORMS OF TOUCH

Making physical contact with another human being can be a great source of comfort. Feeling the physical presence of a person can sometimes touch us in ways that words cannot. Physical contact puts us in direct touch with the presence and quality of another person. We feel the support of his or her body and his or her being. Sometimes words can do this too, but often words get in the way, confuse us, or are misinterpreted. If you are from a family or culture that hugs easily, you will probably find hugging a way of expressing a wide range of emotion—affection, pleasure, comforting, and caring as well as sadness, separation, grief, and loss. In many families, hugging is also a way of greeting or a way of expressing farewell, with all the feelings that accompany these experiences.

In dealing with stress, it is heartwarming not to feel alone. A hug can express support, understanding, and presence. It can be a way of expressing appreciation. In work situations, hugging has not taken on as fast as in the social/family setting, but other forms of touch are becoming more prevalent. A touch on the arm, a grasp of the arm with a handshake, a brief touch of hands, or a more solid holding of a shoulder: All these can let the other person know of your positive presence. An illustration: A supervisor standing behind one of his clerks, who was being verbally attacked by a customer on the other side of a counter, gently touches his subordinate on the shoulder and holds it for a few moments. This let the subordinate know that his supervisor understood what he was experiencing under attack, that he was not alone, and that he had support. A hand on the shoulder of the person sitting alongside you in a tense meeting, when such support would be most appreciated, lets him or her know that you care. In an appropriate situation, a slight squeeze of the shoulder from behind can communicate support and comfort. In the work situation, some of these forms of touch are almost surreptitious. We are still generally uncomfortable about touch at work. It has always interested me how these strange taboos work. Touch is unacceptable at work; but on TV, in front of millions of viewers, one football player pats the bottom of another to show support, and this is quite acceptable!

Some of us, too, were brought up in families or cultures where physical contact (except for spanking) was not modeled. People from these backgrounds often feel uncomfortable with touch, especially with hugging. Men whose fathers did not hug other men may feel very uncomfortable when approached by a "hugger." My father hugged me as a child and right on into adulthood. I am therefore quite comfortable hugging other men. If you, as a man, are not, but wish to become so, it only takes practice. As with anything new (riding a bicycle for the first time), in the beginning it will feel strained, artificial, and difficult. With practice, it will become more natural. This will add to your repertoire still another way of handling your stress.

CRYING

For some people, crying can be a powerful release for pent up stress. Crying and especially sobbing can provide one with some physical release, a form of LMA. Crying ex-presses emotion—it's a form of release; the stress of keeping emotion inside can be released this way.

People who use crying vary in their comfort in doing so. Some of us are uncomfortable because of societal pres-sures about crying. Our society tends to view crying either as an act of immaturity (only babies cry), as a technique to manipulate someone (the stereotype of the "little woman" getting her way through tears), or as a feminine trait (only girls cry). Although we are getting away from these stereo-typed views of crying, many of us are unable to cry or are uncomfortable doing so. I, for one, do not cry, but many men report to me that they are becoming increasingly able to do so and are comfortable in doing it. For those readers who do cry, I would encourage you to feel comfortable about doing so. I truly envy you this opportunity for stress release.

RITUALS, TRADITION, AND ROUTINE

At times of high stress, part of our concern may be caused by the unfamiliar, by a feeling of uncertainty or confusion, or by ambiguity and vagueness. At such times, it may give us considerable comfort to rely on the familiar, the routine, the stable, and the predictable. What remains the same in our lives can indeed help us to face the changing, the un-known, and the stressful. The familiar exists in many forms and traditions in our lives—in ritualistic ways of doing things, in routine activity, and in regular occurrences. Any of these can add stability and provide comfort. With these familiar reoccurrences, we feel more secure and less threat-ened by upheaval.

Most job situations provide the opportunity for routine in some form or another. When things are particularly stressful, a routine activity can help to settle one. Reading time cards, correcting reports for spelling, cleaning up a mess, organizing one's desk or files, and tidying up the work place are all examples. At home, routine activities can provide stability after a particularly trying day: pulling weeds, shoveling snow, sweeping the floor, hosing down the driveway, or watering plants—all relatively routine, easily accomplished tasks. I, for one, like to wash dishes, and many men also use this routine pleasure for relaxation.

We can build tradition into our lives through social and religious areas. Religion offers many opportunities. In the Jewish religion, lighting candles on Friday night carries a powerful mood of the traditional, of roots, of the past, and of the unchanging. All religions have parallel traditions. Sometimes religious traditions recalled from childhood are still capable of evoking positive and comforting emotions. If you gave up these earlier traditions, you may find pleasure and comfort by re-instituting them again in adulthood.

We develop traditions at work and socially as well. Bowling every Monday night, having a special lunch with coworkers every Friday, playing cards every lunch hour, and going out for a drink after a regular monthly meeting with the top boss are all examples. Going somewhere regularly with the same friend or couple—attending a show on its first night, a movie premiere, or an opening at the community art gallery—and doing these things regularly, and especially with the same people, becomes a social tradition.

All these activities are enjoyable and/or socially supporting at the time they occur. They also provide us with two additional pleasures. They provide both future expectations and past memories. We look forward with pleasure to their occurrence, and we look backward with pleasurable memory. Sharing the past is part of the stability and the development of roots. Look for opportunities to develop social and work traditions so that they become part of ones that already exist.

Families develop traditions, usually around holidays but at other times as well. As a child, every Sunday our family met at my Grandmother's house for a family get-together. It was rare that anyone missed it, and it provided that stability and comfort so lacking in many of our lives nowadays. Doing something regularly with the family—perhaps once a week, even if it is brief—can provide some stability; reading to the children every night before bed, going out for hamburgers every Saturday, or having some kind of family music performance together every Sunday evening. In the Mormon religion, for example, one night a week is a family night together. Look for old or new ways you can develop family traditions and see if they can provide more stability for you in times of stress.

SPENDING MONEY

Some of us enjoy spending money during times of high stress. It provides, at the very least, an opportunity to indulge oneself. This need to indulge ourselves might be particularly needful during times when we feel put down or in the dumps. This seems similar to the old bit about the woman who, when she feels depressed, goes out and buys a new hat. Her spirits soar; her morale lifts. Men do this, too. This can be the time when they go out and buy clothing, gadgets, tools, adult toys, and other items. Some of these items we buy are high status items and therefore make us look or feel better. Our self-esteem, at least temporarily, is raised. You can buy expensive things (toys) like stereos, camera equipment, a new car, and the like. These items can raise one's self-esteem. However, many people are satisfied with flea markets, garage sales, and other low cost expenditures. Just "getting a bargain" can make us feel better. Some of us, of course, react negatively to spending money—just the thought of doing it increases our stress. At times, two people in a marriage are in conflict because one is a stress spender, and the other is one who tightens up under high stress. Sometimes talking over these differences and the reasons for the spending helps.

Whether for self-indulgence or to raise our self-esteem, spending money can be helpful to some of us during stressful periods.

PLAYING

There are lots of ways we play and things we play at. However, there is an important distinction about play that might make a difference to you in terms of using play as a stress release.

One kind of play is tense, heavy, and competitive. It is rule ridden and controlled. Examples of this might be the way some of us play card games, such as bridge or poker, or a sport like singles tennis or racquetball. In general, this kind of play is not highly releasing or relieving (see Chapter 20 on Competition for help in identifying this kind of play). You will have to monitor yourself to determine the effects of this on you, but this, in general, is not the quality of play discussed here.

The pleasurable goodie type of play is freer, looser, more improvised, and less organized. Most people, when they recall situations of this kind, use such phrases as "fooling around," "horsing around," "playful," or "fun." We immediately think of tickling, rolling around on the floor, giggling, and spontaneous laughter and joy. We can play around with something or with someone, but no one gets hurt; no one loses. The flow is smooth and spontaneous. We can do this with things—play with a camera or a football or just shoot baskets—or with people—play with the kids or with the "guys at work." The quality is important here in order to achieve a particular kind of stress release (see Chapter 18 on the Me-Act; see also the section on Humor in this chapter if you want additional information).

Some of us adults have difficulty in achieving this play state. We are too serious, and life is too heavy: Play is only for kids. Yet many adults of all ages admit that when they engage in this kind of play, they find it satisfying and see it as a relief from the heavy responsibilities of work and life. You can cultivate this style and become more comfortable with it. One readily available source of help is a child. We talk a great deal about how our children model our adult behavior and about how much of their learning comes from the adults they live with during the first eighteen years of their lives. We learned much from our parents: those "old tapes" and ways of relating and doing things. Instead, how about adults modeling children—the way they behave; their reactions; and, in particular, their use of play? Take a few minutes to observe a child or some children at play. Would any of their behavior be admirable for you to model, helpful in times of stress?

HOT TUBS AND THE LIKE

Here's another method that has ancient roots, as well as sources in a variety of cultures. The approaches and equipment vary—a hot bath, a sauna, a Turkish bath, hot tubs, Jacuzzis, sun baths, sun lamps, or the newly devised "total immersion" tanks—but the essential ingredient in most of these seems to be heat. The heat relaxes our muscles, and here again, our emotions follow suit. People who already know about these approaches need no encouragement. Enthusiasts are usually highly convinced, laudatory, and become missionaries. If you haven't really tried one of these, the next time you're invited, jump right in!

SLEEP

Although the specialists who do research in the scientific study of sleep are not yet clear as to the purposes of sleep, we all do find sleep necessary. Some of us find sleep restful, quieting, and stress reducing. Some people find it easy to sleep, even under high stress. These people describe sleep as a withdrawal or escape, and they awake in a more relaxed, stress-less mood. Others of us are quite the opposite; under high stress, rest is difficult. Disturbances in sleep and rest are just further indications that our stress level is too high. Some individuals then find it difficult to fall asleep; others awaken in the middle of the night (see Chapter 17 on

Solitude). For persons who are concerned about being over-tired, one possible answer is taking rest periods during the day. A rest or cat nap during the day can be a quick rejuve-nator. It should be brief, perhaps fifteen or twenty minutes. Generally, a longer nap leaves one groggy, whereas a brief rest is energizing and renewing. Cat naps can be taken after lunch, upon arriving home from work, and sometimes even at break periods during the day. The problems most of us have with cat naps is finding a comfortable, socially accept-able place to lie down. You may have to be creative about this, depending on your work situation. Until we set up reg-ular "solitude rooms" in offices and plants, you will proba-bly have to hunt for some secluded corner, a quiet lounge, an empty room, even a closet, or possibly a nurse's office. Many older buildings do have secret places tucked away in little-trafficked areas. One item that helps me considerably in attaining cat naps and rest in busy, noisy places is a set of earplugs. They cut out the sound considerably and permit one to withdraw. I use the kind made by hearing aid spe-cialists, which are molded from impressions to fit your own ears.

I've also heard of managers clearing off their desks and lying down right on top of them or using the floor in a cor-ner on a soft rug. If you drive in a carpool, resting (sleeping) while others drive is another possibility (those earplugs really help here). The possibilities are there, the social dis-comfort is generally high, but the rewards might make it worthwhile. As with other self-care activities suggested in this book, you may be able to reduce your discomfort some-what by discussing your needs with your coworkers, boss, or spouse. You may even discover from them some of the hiding places they are using!

This chapter includes a variety of possibilities. These choices are especially personal. What are the pleasurable, self-indulgent goodies that work for you? How could you incorporate more of them into your busy, active life?

RECALL REMINDER

**PLEASURABLE
GOODIES**

Check the following pleasurable goodies you would like
to use more:

_____ Music.

_____ Laughter.

_____ Prayer.

_____ Poetry.

_____ Apologize—to whom?_____

_____ Hugging—who?_____

_____ Crying.

_____ Rituals—what kind?_____

_____ Buying things.

_____ Play.

_____ Hot baths.

_____ Rest—where?_____

When do I want to begin some of these?

14

SUPPORT GROUPS

Dick belongs to a group at church that meets every Wednesday night. It's not a large group—usually ten to fifteen people attend each week—but many of the same people have attended for a number of years. They do a variety of things related to church activity, everything from fund raising to driving the youth groups on field trips to even helping in some church remodeling and repairs. Over the years, there's been lots of time in between the church related activities to develop feelings of closeness for each other. At times, they have let their hair down, shared their lives, kidded around with each other, and kept in touch. Almost without Dick realizing it, this group has become an important source of support for him. He gets regular enjoyment from it; he leans on it and looks forward to it. It's a group of people he regularly sees, feels comfortable with, and feels close to. All are very valuable sources of support in times of stress.

Support groups exist in so many kinds and forms and affiliations that it's sometimes confusing to identify what the basic ingredients are. Some of the necessary factors seem to be the following: (1) The same people attend; (2) the group meets regularly (once a week seems ideal); (3) the group has met for a fair period of time (until closeness develops); and (4) there is an opportunity for informality, for spontaneity, and for indidental contacts. What kinds of groups meet these requirements? Here's a sample:

An informal group of coworkers.

A formal coworker group, for example, a weekly luncheon group, a monthly management organization, an executive club, and the like.

A sports or hobby group, for example, a singing group, a square dance club, a racquetball club, and the like.

One's own large, kinship family (there are still some around).

An activity group, for example, a weekly discussion, book reading, play reading, and the like.

Service group (Kiwanis, Rotary, etc., and especially small informal satellite shoot-offs from these large groups).

Extended families (artificial, intentional families developed in churches, community organizations, etc.).

Racial, ethnic, and nationality groups (associations, clubs, etc.).

Vocational groups (organized and formal).

Church and other community groups.

Strictly social groups, for example, singles clubs, men's group, women's consciousness raising groups, and the like.

Perhaps there are others that you can identify in your own life. Your use of these groups for support can, of course, be developed. Possibly you have, at present, only peripheral or past membership in a group. You may decide to seek more support in that group. You can do that by involving yourself more in the group and by encouraging activities that permit or foster closeness.

It's my belief that the stated activity of the group is not particularly important for developing closeness as long as you meet the basic requirements—that is, see the same people, regularly and over a period of time, and have peripheral opportunities to develop closeness. People do develop closeness during the activity itself (while playing cards, racquetball, reading plays, raising funds, etc.), but much more closeness is usually developed from the interactions that are only incidental to the goal activity. The incidental opportunities include the following:

Driving to and from meetings with someone.
Having dinner together before or after the meetings.
Having a group potluck meal.
Meeting in someone's house.
Talking during coffee breaks, in the social get-together after the "formal" meeting.
Chats, separate social get-togethers, and the like.
Solving problems and making decisions together.
Pairing up outside the group with another group member.
Going on a trip together, to a convention, or to a retreat setting.

If the group is too formal to allow for the above kinds of interactions, little closeness may develop. If you want more closeness in a group you belong to, you might plan one or more of the above "incidentals."

In summary, you may want to explore either joining a group for support purposes or using groups you already belong to for achieving more closeness. It may be, too, that your social support system is comprised of a number of individuals who do not belong to the same group (see Chapter 9 on venting). In this event, you may feel sufficient closeness without the necessity for group membership. One way or the other, check out your social support system as another valuable asset in times of stress.

RECALL REMINDER

14

SUPPORT GROUPS

I want to gain some more support and closeness. I will join or attend more regularly the following groups:

_____

_____

_____

I can also increase closeness by engaging in incidental activities, such as the following:

_____

_____

_____

_____

15

HUMAN PAIN

After being introduced to the concept of the Do-nut (see Chapter 8), some individuals begin to rethink their views on the human condition of pain. Because hurt or pain is seen as the underlying cause of anger, now one has a choice—a choice between experiencing those painful underlying feelings or turning them into anger. Because of this choice, persons who accept the idea of the Do-nut in theory sometimes have difficulty in accepting it in practice. Their point of view is aptly put, "Sometimes the hurt hurts more than getting angry, so I'd rather get angry."

If the pain, for example, involves being afraid we might fail in our work, or finding it painful to be ignored by our boss, or if our job makes us feel painfully insignificant and unimportant, why face those painful feelings if anger is available to us? Rather than experience pain, at times it may seem that anger is the easiest way to go—and by far the more comfortable method. Certainly it's less painful than feeling inadequacy, rejection, insignificance, and uselessness.

Whether you should or should not get angry is, of course, your choice. Although I sometimes still get angry, I have made the decision against anger. Some readers, for any of the reasons discussed earlier, may have made a similar commitment. You may have rejected anger and negative behavior in your life. After this decision, you then have the problem of facing those painful underlying feelings—those feelings of rejection, loss, inadequacy, helplessness, and the like.

Painful though this process is, you do have numerous options available to you. The process of facing those feelings can be viewed as a defusing process. We want to lower the intensity of the pain without denying the hurt. We want to face the pain without needing to cover it up with negative behaviors toward ourselves and others.

We can accomplish this defusing of painful emotions by any number of techniques described in this part of the book—for example, LMA, the muscle relaxation methods and the Me-Act described in Chapter 18. Also, time is , of course, the great healer. If you are able to leave the painful situation for a while, the pain will slowly ebb away. Using these techniques can sometimes shorten the healing time. Occasionally the suffering can even be considerably reduced.

If we decide to face our pain, any of the above emotion-lowering approaches can also be of help. Consider also techniques that bring out your hurting or uncomfortable feelings. For example, share or vent your pain to your listening spouse or friend (Chapter 9) or even to a counselor or therapist, use your support group (Chapter 14), verbalize your hurting feelings to the person you feel "caused it" (Chapter 8—the Do-nut), or rely on your personal therapies (Chapter 13). Although there is no simple, easy answer, all these approaches can make it somewhat easier (and sometimes considerably so) to face your painful feelings and to understand and accept them.

It's somewhat of a cliché that we can learn from pain, but let's take a look at some of the possibilities in becoming a better person through the way we deal with our painful feelings:

1. We can learn something about ourselves, about what we need from people, and about the way we relate to people. For example, "My boss' feelings are more important to me than I realized".

2. We can become more sensitive to suffering and pain in others. We can grow in our ability to empathize and to understand the other person's point of view. We develop our compassion. We can truly say, "I understand".

3. We can learn about our limitations and, in some instances, take steps to reduce them. In our jobs, for example, we can learn new ways of handling situations we dealt with badly, or we can take courses to increase our knowledge and skills.

4. Sometimes the pain can motivate us to change a situation for the better. We change rules, procedures, and laws. What causes the pain then no longer exists. Often, this helps others. Probably a great deal of social change results from this use of pain.

5. We develop some religious, spiritual, or other meaning from the suffering in our lives that can aid us in future situations.*

One special source of pain that we may identify by using the Do-nut is a feeling of helplessness, powerlessness, or impotency. This feeling is frequently mentioned as arising out of work situations.† For example:

"I've tried everything I can to change the situation, and nothing works."
"I have no control over issues that are vitally important to me."

---

*More on this later as we discuss Viktor Frankl's views on suffering.
†This feeling is also not unusual for parents of teen-agers. In the small city in which I live, the local newspaper recently reported that parents of over one hundred runaway teen-agers last year told police that they couldn't cope with their children, that they found them impossible, and that they didn't want them returned home.

"My superior (boss, etc.) is adamant, impossible, and
    so on."
"State (or Federal) laws make this intolerable."
"There's no money in the budget."
"So and so is unapproachable."
"The issue is not negotiable."
"Rules and regulations cannot be modified."
"Bureaucratic inertia prevents change."

We have applied our energies to change the situation;
all our skills and abilities have been used. The result: The
situation remains unchanged, we have failed, and an additional hurt has been added to the inside of the Do-nut. We
feel a loss of control, a powerlessness, a helplessness. It may
hurt a great deal to feel these feelings, to face them, and to
admit them.

What can be done in these work or family situations to
ease this particular painful feeling? Again, we do have the
option of becoming angry, defensive, or blaming. We also
have all the emotion-lowering techniques mentioned earlier. Sometimes just lowering your emotional temperature
to reasoning and reasonable levels results in your becoming
aware again of new alternatives, of solutions, or of a way
out. Your brain is operating again, and your intelligence is
available to you. You then find a way out of your powerlessness.

Sometimes none of this seems to help; the situation is
indeed hopeless. We feel trapped. Perhaps, before despair
sets in, we can learn something from Viktor Frankl's experience (Frankl, 1963). Frankl was a psychiatrist who was held
prisoner in a concentration camp during World War II. Certainly none of our job experiences can more forcefully contribute to a feeling of powerlessness than being an inmate in
a Nazi concentration camp during the holocaust years of
1939–1945—being held a prisoner against one's will, under
conditions of starvation, disease, and dying, surrounded by
torture, suicide, and the ever present horror of mass murder

in the gas ovens hovering over one's daily existence. Yet Frankl's conclusion is as follows:

> *Man can preserve a vestige of spiritual freedom, of independence of mind even in such terrible conditions of psychic and physical stress. . . . Everything can be taken from a man but one thing: the last of human freedoms—to choose one's attitude [my emphasis] in any given set of circumstances, to choose one's own way.*

The lesson for us is clear. When all other options are taken away, we still have one option—the option of changing our *attitude*, or our view of the situation and thereby even behaving differently.

What new attitudes can you develop to help ease your powerless feelings at work? Look for opportunities in your job where you can still be independent, where you can, in spite of all restrictions, express your basic values and beliefs. Within your limits of freedom, how can you be the kind of person you want to be?

Recognize, too, that you are not 100 percent powerless, that you always (even in a concentration camp) have the power to change yourself. This alone reduces the intensity of pain and makes it more bearable. I recall a situation in my own life where this was dramatically illustrated. I had, within the space of a year, experienced public humiliation and job failure (my job performance was attacked twice a day in the newspapers), and in the same year, I experienced a painful divorce and separation from my children. By the end of that year, I felt rejected, humiliated, helpless, and a host of other depressing feelings. I was unable to shake these painful feelings. I was really in a downer. At the time, I was teaching in a college in a part of the country where it snowed a great deal. I remember the snow vividly, because one day, walking on the snow-covered campus, it suddenly dawned on me that I was not helpless, that I had not been done in by the world, that I did contribute to my situation in the past, and that I therefore had the power to get out of it. This sudden change of attitude was the boost that started me on the way up.

To take another example: One of the more difficult problems parents face is an older child who persistently wets his or her bed. Parents try every method to change this behavior and often fail in the effort. The situation seems hopeless. They are powerless. When they reach this feeling of helplessness, they often change their attitude about the situation—accepting it instead of fighting it. Often, the result is that the child gives up the bed-wetting.

When nothing else can be changed, we still have one very large option available to us: We can change our own attitudes. Frankl developed a whole system of psychotherapy out of his personal use of his concept. In recent years, counseling of persons who are dying, even those with terminal cancer, and couseling of persons with irreparable loss, such as widows, are other examples of the basic concept of attitude change in the face of unalterable circumstances. This concept, too, might be of help to you in facing some of that pain you will inevitably face as a human being.

RECALL REMINDER

15

HUMAN PAIN

What defusing techniques can I use to lessen my hurt (see page 147).

What can I try to learn from my recent hurts? (see the list on pages 147–148)

What intolerable situations could I make more tolerable by changing my attitude?

TAKING CARE
OF YOURSELF

GUILT

For many of us, just the tentative thought of self-care can arouse uncomfortable feelings. If we go further and actually consider nurturing or nourishing ourselves, it can get downright uncomfortable. Proceed further, and think specifically about taking time for *yourself*: using your own lunch hour for personal self-renewal or taking time from your family for your own personal enjoyment. What's your reaction to these suggestions? For some of us, these thoughts alone make us twist and squirm. Can you visualize that disapproving, threatening, pointing puritan in yourself whose duty lies in keeping you on the right track of the work ethic? Upholder of those values now considered old-fashioned—duty, responsibility, dedication, tradition— even loyalty and honor? And think, too, of the boss or your spouse catching you—horrors!

Most of us are severely conscientious in our work. We are responsible in our jobs; we feel a sense of duty to perform as best we can.

In contrast, however, when it comes to self-care, most of us feel considerably less dedication and sense of duty. We could never allow ourselves to neglect our jobs in the ways we flagrantly neglect the daily care of our emotions, of our mental condition, and of our bodies. Persons who consider themselves conscientious and responsible take care of themselves in ways that are typically casual, even haphazard, largely irresponsible. These are attitudes most of us could not tolerate in taking care of our work or our families.

This neglect of self-care is especially evident when work pressures increase and, therefore, when time becomes scarce. During these particularly stressful periods, many of us take even less time for self-care than we do normally. When things get rough, our typically inadequate self-care activity often becomes completely nonexistent. "I don't have time for myself" is often heard.

A basic premise of Part Three of this book emphasizes that when pressures, demands, and deadlines increase, we have a greater need to deal with our emotions, to change our mental states, and to rid ourselves of the tension in our bodies—basically to lower our stress to more reasonable and productive levels. The paradox of self-care is obvious: *We need to take the time for self-care most when the least time is available.*

The root of this problem for many of us lies in our attitudes about taking care of ourselves and in our attitudes about work. When you were brought up, do you remember being clearly told, "You don't go out to play until you get your homework done?" Do you recall, "The chores get done first?" Many adults can still sense this kind of attitude in themselves. You are not allowed to relax, enjoy yourself, or even take the time to rest, until your work is done-All of your work. And when, pray tell me, in your job will you ever get all that work done? When, at home, will you get through with all the jobs around the house that need doing? And the things you should do with your kids or the time to spend with your spouse? Still, the attitude prevails: discomfort, a sense of wrongness, and feelings of guilt. The job comes first: Take care of the troops first. Self-sacrifice to meet the needs of others. Then and only then, find time for yourself. And there never is time.

Do you spend lunch hour for yourself, for your own renewal, and for restoring your emotions so that you may better and more productively face your afternoon's work? When you do that, do you feel guilty or afraid that someone (the boss or your coworkers) will find out? Do you ever spend your coffee breaks on personal nurturance rather than social chit-chat? Do you feel uncomfortable about separating from your fellow workers and not joining them for the sociability of the office? Do fellow workers joke about "goofing off" if anyone dares mention his or her needs for quiet, solitude, or renewal time? Do you feel guilty or uncomfortable over mentioning to people at work (your boss or your supervisor) that you have needs? Are you uncomfortable or feeling guilty about taking time from the family for yourself? Do you feel heavily your responsibilities as a father or mother or as a husband or wife? Or as a child? For those of you plagued by these uncomfortable feelings, and most of us seem at least mildly susceptible to such discomfort, I have a special psychological definition for this kind of guilt. The psychological definition of guilty feelings aroused when one considers self-care is:

GUILT = SHIT

I hope I haven't offended anyone, but the word has been chosen with great care. We all know what to do with that stuff, and that's what we should do with our guilt—flush it!

As you rid yourself of your guilt, all sorts of possibilities emerge. Here's one: Peter had a report due on his boss' desk at eight o'clock the next morning. It was the first task on his priority list for today, but he barely even got the time to look at it. It was one of those days—telephone calls, problems, complaints, and emergencies all day long. Five o'clock arrived. Peter was weary. The report, unfinished, lay on his desk. Normally, at that hour, he would put his nose to the grindstone and grind out that report. Peter, however, recalled the psychological definition of guilt, left the office, and went home. He took his wife out to a movie and had dinner. At 9:00 at night, he sat down with that report, and, to his amazement, he completed that report in less than thirty minutes. And it was an excellent job. Peter was brought up with the dictum, "Homework first, and only then are you allowed to play." Sometimes we need to play first in order to do a good job on our homework.

Monitor yourself and recognize when you need nurturing, renewal, and a change of pace. You may well find, as Peter did, that the results are higher performance, better quality work, and faster, more efficient work output.

Some of us now have a "mental health" day or a personal day off—a recognition that we all need time just to put ourselves together. I have heard of parents who allowed their children any five days off from school during the school year—no explanations necessary—just for renewal and recharging. Letting the child choose the days helps him or her learn to self-monitor more accurately and reduces the need to get "sick" in order to deal with stress.

Many women report having special trouble with guilt. Women, up until recently (is it *still* going on in your family?), were brought up to take care of and to nurture both men and children. Many women tell me that during their upbringing, subordinating their own needs was the automatic order of things. Feed the men and the children first, take care of them, listen to them, comfort them, clean up after them, and so on. Actually, the old-fashioned self-sacrificing mother was a fraud. She never gave it away for nothing. She exacted quite a bit in return, and when her children grew up (if she let them), they were unwilling to continue to give her what she demanded. We can sacrifice and deny our needs, and this is part of love. But we can do this at best only temporarily, and we can't do it very well (if at all) when our stress level mounts. We only fool ourselves if we think that we are caring for others and doing a good job at it while our own emotional, mental, and physical needs are being ignored. Sooner or later it gets to us, resentment sets in, or we fall to pieces.

Denying one's own needs can take place in both sexes, in a work situation as well as in the family. Learning to say "no" and to become more assertive about oneself are useful for both men and women who are ready to move out of this self-defeating style of self-sacrifice (see references on assertiveness training).

Get rid of your guilt. This is an attitude you have to conquer in yourself. Some aids follow:

1. Recognize that everyone needs time for self-care (even Superman at the office). Your spouse or boss may get it at a different time of day than you, but we all need it. If you are uncomfortable with this at work or in your family, talking it over often helps. The other person may need reassurance that you are not goofing off or rejecting them (especially spouses). Ask for their suggestions: you'll probably hear from them how they manage or wish they could manage their own stress. After a discussion of this kind, most persons feel more free about taking the inevitable time for self-care.

2. Remember that the purpose of self-care is to make you a better employee—or a better father or mother or spouse or partner. Check it out. Do you do a better job after taking the time for self-care? Are you more patient and understanding with others? Self-monitor again.

3. Time for self-care is rarely given to you. "Take an hour off" is not often heard from either a boss or a spouse. You have to take it, to schedule it, possibly seize it. Refer to paragraph number five.

4. If you neglect self-care or push too hard, self-monitor the results in yourself: Check out your feelings, your total behaviors and performance, and your body. Make the judgment: Is this the kind of employee, worker, spouse, or parent I really want to be?

5. Consider reading a book or taking a course in assertiveness training. One of the books is aptly called, *When I Say No, I Feel Guilty* (Smith, 1975). Learn to feel more comfortable about saying "no" and learn how to do it nicely—to coworkers, customers, clients, and taxpayers; to spouses and children; even to your boss!

6. When appropriate, recall the psychological definition of guilt. You know how to handle that stuff. Actually, don't handle it—just dump it!

RECALL REMINDER

16

GUILT

When do I need to be reminded of the psychological definition of guilt (check if appropriate):

_____With certain people—who?_____

_____In certain situations:_____

_____With the boss.

_____Daily or frequently.

_____Sometimes or occasionally.

17
SOLITUDE

John drove home from work through the usual rush hour traffic. He felt weary, but his mind was quite active. He recalled the kind of day it had been as he weaved or waited through the traffic. Several deadlines were due that day, a project he completed weeks ago was returned for a lengthy revision, and several irate customers had to be dealt with on the phone; there was one mild criticism from his superior, a new problem with a job he was preparing, and old problems with a subordinate he supervises. There were also some satisfactions and some joys. A hectic, busy day—a stressful one. As he approached home, John became aware that his wife would be waiting, looking forward to his arrival on the home scene. She would be waiting to greet him and to share some experiences of her day. She probably wanted to seek some closeness with him. Inevitably, they would have to discuss that recurrent problem they were having with their fifteen-year-old son. As he walked up to the door, he could already hear the loud rock music on the stereo. He braced himself. He didn't really want to face any of this. He desperately wanted nothing more than to be alone: to talk to no one and to listen to no one. He didn't want to be assaulted by any voices or by any music. He wanted to sit alone, possibly read the paper or look at a magazine, have a drink, or maybe watch TV. But he just wanted to be alone.

Solitude, for most of us, is vital to our well-being and is absolutely required for coping with the daily stress of work and living.

There seem to be many reasons for this. Let's take a closer look at why people find solitude so rewarding. This may help us to recognize the full scope of the solitude experience.

Individuals most frequently report that solitude removes them from all those external stressors of work and family. They get away from the demands of bosses, spouses, children, customers, taxpayers, or students; from those who complain or are angry; from those expectations that need to be satisfied; and from people who want to be heard. Cutting off all that external stimulation seems to be a first necessary step in the reduction of stress. Remember that cartoon you've seen in so many offices of those giggly, playful creatures who are laughingly saying, "What, you want it done today?" We get too many demands and too many pressures. Kay works behind a counter and she says, "I don't want to listen to anyone, to talk to anyone, or to hear one more request or complaint." George is an engineer and deals with problems all day. He says, "I have to get away from the barrage. I want peace; I want quiet; I want to be alone."

Related to this is an intense need not to interact with anyone—to get away from any social contact. This can be particularly important for supervisors and managers who typically deal with people all day. Many of us work in "people" jobs. Most professional positions are people jobs, too. If it's people all day long, we desperately need time to be away from people—even people we care about. John, at the beginning of this chapter, feels this need. He doesn't even want to be with his wife, whom he loves. Being around someone you love can be felt as a pressure. Because we love him or her and are considerate of him or her, we think about and consider him or her. We find it difficult to care for him or her and to care for ourselves at the same time. During solitude times, many people report the need to be away from all social contacts, even loving ones.

Many individuals report that the importance of solitude for them is in its renewal value. In order to face future responsibilities at work or in the family, solitude offers a recharging experience. The result is facing responsibility more comfortably, along with more productive working on our tasks. Time away from our families can result in more loving and caring feelings when we return. Bill gets this kind of solitude time while driving home from work. He drives mainly on the freeway, and his attention easily wanders from the driving to contemplating the work day he has just experienced. He reflects on it, considers it, and gets it out of his system. After this kind of relaxed thinking, Bill finds it easier to face his family when he arrives home. Mary is a teacher's aide and she feels fortunate in that she gets home from her work one hour earlier than her own children return from school. She needs this hour "to put herself together" before she faces her children, her husband, and her responsibilities. How does she spend the time? "Nothing special—possibly a little housework. Sometimes I read the paper or plan supper; mostly, I just sit relaxed, reflecting on my work day, considering possibilities, and making some decisions for tomorrow." Jack feels the need for this kind of renewal in the middle of the day, during his lunch hour. He goes for walks around the neighborhood where he works, and he walks alone. For twenty or thirty minutes, he has the opportunity to be alone with himself in a relaxing, easygoing walk. Jack says, "I can face the afternoon better; I'm more relaxed and calmer. It also gives me a different perspective on the morning. . . . I'm not so uptight about what bothered me before lunch." Jack deliberately uses solitude to recharge himself for the rest of the day's work.

Many people, when they describe their solitude, use words that reveal the thinking/contemplative quality of the experience. We do need time to think! Surprisingly, it seems very difficult for most employees to think at work. No matter what their position or their professional stature, most individuals report that it's nearly impossible to think on the job. In fact, in most work situations, it is literally socially unacceptable to think while at work. Just consider your own work situation for a moment. If your work involves physical labor and you stop to think about what you are doing, what sort of reaction do you get from your fellow workers? Why, you are goofing off, of course, and someone, however jokingly, will let you know that. But even if you work at a desk, if someone comes by and sees you without a pen or pencil or telephone in your hand or no book or paper before you, what's their impression of what you are doing? Why, you're not working, of course: You're not busy, you're available to be interrupted, or (possibly) you're even wasting your time. Many managers sheepishly admit that they close their office doors in order to think. At times, they even feel uncomfortable doing that.

What kind of thinking requires solitude? The terms people use to describe their thinking rather aptly reveal what's going on: reflecting, contemplating, evaluating, fantasizing, or possibly meditating. "Putting the day together" may well involve reflecting on such things as, "How did I handle that situation with the boss?" "What are the effects of the way I dealt with that customer?" "What could I have done differently in reprimanding that subordinate?" "What can I do tomorrow to follow up, to make amends, or to reinforce what I did today?" Along with this kind of thinking we inevitably fantasize things we "might have done" or "wished we had done." At times, we try to patch up or put our self-esteem back together. Inevitably, too, we rehearse the future. We do this in our efforts to do better, to be more successful, or to be more productive. These are all powerful thinking uses of solitude. They are necessary to our handling of typical daily stresses.

Another kind of thinking activity that individuals describe is priority setting. This kind of thinking demands solitude. Priority thinking is related to such questions as the following: "Who am I?" "What's important to me?" "How do I want to spend my time and use my talents and abilities?" Kay says she finds it difficult to get her priorities established in the presence of her husband or her male boss. She says, "From childhood, I learned that the woman's role is to please the man and to subordinate herself to him. I'm trying to get out of this, but it's easier to get my thinking straight when I sit alone and decide for myself what's important to me." When we are in the presence of significant or loving others, our priority thinking can become confused, and this can muddle up our decision making. This can happen to me when my wife is present and we are trying to make a simple decision—what to do tonight? I automatically consider her opinions as well as my own. So "what's important to me" gets confused with "what's important to my wife." I lose my clarity; I am no longer sure whether I really want to go out for dinner, go to the movies, or just stay home. In the job, this can happen in the presence of fellow workers, status persons, and particularly the boss. Solitude becomes necessary for gaining an answer to those job identity questions: "What do I feel is the right way to handle that problem?" "What ability do I have to offer in working on that project?" "How do I think I should develop that report or handle that dissatisfied customer?" The power of solitude again!

With so many needs for solitude, busy people have been most creative about finding times during the day for getting in some solitude time.

Mary sets her alarm one hour earlier than she has to. She does this every day she works. She gets up before the rest of the family and has a whole hour to herself. How does she spend the time? "Looking at the morning paper, slowly sipping a cup of coffee, thinking about the coming day and how I want to deal with some problems coming up." Mary says, "I don't like getting to work rushed and harried; at least I start the day relaxed." The early morning is often quiet and in many households is a good time for peace and solitude. Some people are early morning people, too, and they like to get up early.

During the day, opportunities for solitude include coffee breaks, travel time for those who move about in their jobs, and lunch time. People who travel in their work, such as repair persons, agriculture inspectors, salesmen, and the like can often stop for breaks at pleasant places like parks or beaches and use these for solitude. Using coffee breaks requires special effort to resist social interaction. It helps a great deal to have places in the building for solitude. I have been encouraging organizations to establish "solitude lounges" in every building. If possible, these would be separate from typical social lounges, lunch rooms, or rest room areas. In some cases, a part of a lunch room or lounge could be sectioned off with small solitude cubicles. Every building usually has a small unused room somewhere that could be easily adapted for solitude purposes. Inexpensive, restful partitioning with one comfortable chair or couch in each cubicle is all that's required. As solitude becomes more socially acceptable, it is easier for individuals to resist the pressure of social interaction when they desperately need to be alone.

Driving time has already been mentioned as an opportunity used by many of us for solitude. Safety can be an issue here. With most freeway driving, many people find it difficult to concentrate fully on the task of driving. Whether they plan it that way or not, they do find their minds wandering from the driving and do use the time for solitude purposes.

A solitude break of some sort between work and family responsibilities can be developed in other ways as well. Read Chapter 18 on the Me-Act for possibilities here.

Further along in the twenty-four-hour period, some people get their solitude late at night. They stay up after everyone else has gone to sleep. This is used for any and all solitude purposes and often also involves one of the Me-Act activities described in Chapter 18.

To complete the twenty-four-hour period, some of us get solitude time in the middle of the night. Sometimes, we are so tired that we fall asleep but find ourselves awakening at two or three or four in the morning. Something is on our minds; our bodies refuse to sleep. I used to think it was insomnia, and I tried to get the old body to go back to sleep again. I came to realize that I needed to get up just to be alone with myself. The night is a very peaceful, quiet time. It provides me with the opportunity to think, to dream, or to rehearse. Sometimes, too, it gives me time for a little physical activity if I have missed out on that during the day. Sometimes I use the night for an activity, but usually I am just quiet and with myself. If this happens to you, next time it does, consider whether you have awakened because you have not had enough (or any) solitude time during the previous day. Some people report that when they miss several days of solitude, this inevitably results in waking up at night. Perhaps our bodies have more sense than we do, and we certainly should listen to them more!

There are some few people who report that they don't need (or want) time to be alone. I'm not sure whether they are truly missing opportunities for renewal time or not. As I have emphasized before, we are all different, and what works for one may not work for others. If you are one of these persons, you might, however, try some solitude just to see if it can enrich your renewal experience. The many optional uses of solitude may even open up some new possibilities for you. And then, of course, it may not. You might not need it.

Some of you live alone or work alone. Occasionally, people in this position report more solitude time than they want. This seems to be related, of course, to the issue of loneliness. Loneliness is an experience we all have to cope with, whether we are around people or not. I can feel terribly lonely even after a terribly hectic "people day." However, if you feel you have enough solitude, check first to see if you are using solitude well. The solitude rewards described in this chapter may open up new options for you. But then, too, it may be that you just need to be with people in more meaningful, closer, or more intimate relationships (see Chapter 14 on support groups).

In summary, it seems that most of us need time by ourselves. We need to patch ourselves up and put ourselves together after the typical social barrage of life. For many, this seems to be a daily need. As with all self-care activities, we will probably find that we must schedule it in advance. Perhaps more significant is the need to be firm with others in order to seize our solitude. We may need considerable strength in order to resist surrender to social pressures. Often, discussing this issue with others reveals that they, too, need solitude time but that they are getting it at a different time of the day. John's wife gets her solitude time while John is at work. By the time he arrives home, she is bursting with social needs. John talked this over with his wife. She came to realize that what he so desperately needed was what she was getting all day. She no longer felt rejected. John felt less guilty about retreating to his chair and burying himself in his newspaper. Discussion between spouses often results in increased appreciation of the other's stress.

On the job, discussion helps, too. Often, talking about solitude needs with subordinates, secretarial staff, and the like opens up the same increase in understanding. Let's provide, too, more places at work for solitude.

How about children in school? Don't they need solitude time, too? How about in the home, within the family? The open architecture of many of our homes makes retreats to the bathroom or bedroom almost a necessity in the search for solitude. Many mothers with little children report that locking themselves in the bathroom is the only way they get tc be alone. I've heard employees say this, too. They go to the toilet, lock themselves in, and get a little peace and quiet. In our family, we use the term "alone time." Almost from birth, we "brainwash" our children with the concept of alone time. You need it; I need it; Mommy needs it. We want them to understand our needs and their own needs for solitude, and we don't want them to feel rejected when someone wants to be alone.

Remember, too, that alone time can be combined with muscle release (see Chapter 12), LMA (see Chapter 7), some of the pleasurable goodies (see Chapter 13), and so on. The same half-hour walk can be a Me-Act, an opportunity for some physical release of stress, and a time to be alone. Vive la solitude!

RECALL REMINDER

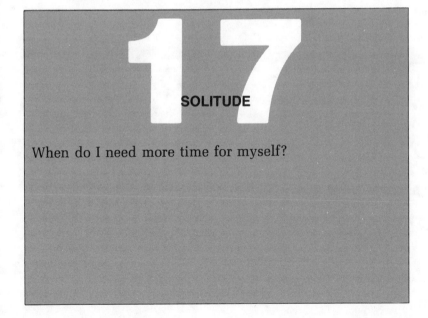

SOLITUDE

When do I need more time for myself?

Where do I get it?

18

THE ME-ACT

Joe gets a great vacation—once a year. He gets three weeks off and really makes a go of it. The family plans for months ahead. They always take off in their camper. They want to get away from it all. Some years, they head for a special place. Other years, they just wander. Joe likes to hunt up old railroads that are still running. He also likes to fish. Sometimes, he just loafs. It's certainly a neat change from his job responsibilities. He does just what he feels like doing, not what he has to do. No bosses, no customers, and no deadlines. It's really relaxing. When he gets back, he can't understand why he got so up tight about certain things before he left. His perspective is completely different. His stress level is considerably lowered. He usually approaches tasks differently, more creatively, and with more energy.

Vacations and holidays are neat. So why not have them more often? Why not every day? It can be done. It does take careful planning. Planning is important, because time each day is so scarce and so easily lost. If we can squeeze twenty to thirty minutes out of a busy work/family day, how can we best use it? In that short a time, what kind of vacation can most effectively reduce stress and renew us?

I call this type of mini-vacation a *Me-Act*. And to use a Me-Act most effectively, two basic rules must be followed. These are as follows:

1. You must do it alone.
2. You must not set specific goals for yourself.

This is perhaps best illustrated in Figure 18–1.

A typical heavy work schedule is represented in diagram A in Figure 18–1. At work, the self is bombarded with expectations from bosses, deadlines, demands from others (customers, taxpayers, students, etc.), interruptions for help or for service, and pressures of all kinds to produce. Each arrow bombarding the self requires us to act—in effect, to *Re-Act* to the bombardment. Most of these expectations are from the outside, but some are self-imposed. These are our stressors!

If this is your typical working day, you may want an antidote of just the opposite kind of experience, a *Me-Act*, as pictured in diagram B in Figure 18–1. In the Me-Act, we do the controlling: We decide what we are going to do. We decide how long we are going to do it and when we are going to stop. We do this on the basis of our interest, our

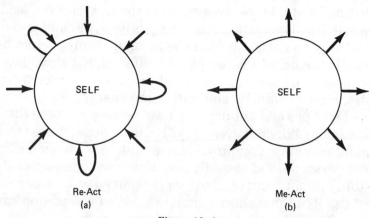

Re-Act
(a)

Me-Act
(b)

Figure 18–1

emotions, and our restfulness. The Me-Act is purely self-propelled.

Dick has developed a neat Me-Act that he does every day. Dick spends twenty minutes of his lunch hour going for a meandering walk. Often, he walks near department stores and other shops. Typically, he just walks and looks at the window displays. As his mood directs him, he may drop into a store and browse in the hardware department. While there, he just casually looks at tools and other gadgets. Once in a while, he varies this with some enjoyable people watching. If it's warm enough, he sits under a tree in a small park near his work and feeds the squirrels. This twenty-minute mini-vacation relaxes him considerably. He looks at whatever he wants to, stops when he wants to, and turns to something else that interests him when he wants to. He stays with it as long as he likes and moves on when he likes.

Dick finds that this reduces the stress he builds up during the morning work. He goes back to the office for the afternoon in a calmer mood, feeling good emotionally. He faces the problems he left from the morning with a new point of view. He's less up tight about them. He benefits from a brief period of vacation, a Me-Act where he has control.

Dick meets the two basic rules for the Me-Act ideally in his mini-vacation. One, Dick does this alone. He resists all efforts at social interaction. He doesn't want to react to anyone. He doesn't have to contend with anyone, to listen to anyone or to look at what interests someone else. He attends only to what he wants to. He controls instead of Re-Acting. Secondly, he has no specific goal. He does not visit a store for a specific purchase. A goal to purchase something instead of browsing would set up a stress situation for him, particularly if there was some problem or delay in what he was buying. He's had enough Re-Act all morning. His meandering and browsing are not completely aimless. But they are completely devoid of any specific goal that must be accomplished during that twenty minutes. He has had a mini-vacation.

Daily Me-Acts can be experienced through a variety of vacation-like actitivities. The quality of these Me-Acts is best described by such words as the following:

Loafing.
Browsing.
Wandering.
Puttering.
Messing about.
Playing.

Let's take each of these descriptive words in turn and explore the possibilities.

Do you *loaf* on vacation? What do you do when you loaf: read, work crossword puzzles, knit, look at the clouds, or go for lazy walks? If these activities meet the two rules for the Me-Act, they can serve admirably for a mini-vacation. One: Do you do these loafing activities alone? Two: Have you avoided specific goals?

Let's take a look at reading, for example. If you are a reader, you probably read alone; but if you read material related to your work, it is undoubtedly goal oriented. This would not be a Me-Act. Many readers report that for Me-Acts they read what they call "junk" books: cheap novels, science fiction, mysteries, westerns, gothics, and the like. Some get into more heavy reading, but only in a slow, goalless fashion. How about you crossword puzzle fiends—do you have a specific goal? John does crossword puzzles for relaxation during his coffee breaks. I ask John, what if you don't finish the puzzle today or tomorrow? He says, "No bother, I can always work on it again some other time." He's not up tight about accomplishing anything. His goal is not specific. If he had to find all the words or finish it either before the break was up or by the end of the day, it would be stressful. Then, of course, it would not be a Me-Act.

Stop for a moment and list your loafing activities, thereby making them more available to you. Recall all the lazy, aimless, taking-it-easy, and relaxing things you like to do. How many of these could you fit in, somehow, every day?

If you don't loaf, perhaps you *browse*. Browsing is a neat way to gain a Me-Act. Where do you browse? Jane loves to browse in department stores. Sometimes, she drops in to the kitchen or housewares departments; at other times, some gadget demonstration attracts her. Some days, she likes to look at clothes, shoes, or cosmetics. Fortunately, her office is downtown in a large city, and the possibilities are endless. She does it alone and does not use her lunch hour for shopping. Shopping would set up a pressure for her and would not be a Me-Act. Mike is in a different spot. He loves antiques. He works in a plant in the suburbs near a freeway. Whenever he can, he drives to an antique shop and just browses. He gets to do this more on weekends, but on the way home from work, he may deliberately plan to visit one or two antique shops, just for browsing. This Me-Act helps him to decompress from work and to return home less stressful. At times, he skips his lunch (or just eats an apple or two) and spends his lunch hour driving to an antique shop and browsing. He says that he feels better emotionally and physically all afternoon.

Just about any interest could be turned into a *browsing* or *wandering* type of Me-Act: nature; woods; the beach; shops of any kind (hobby shops, bike shops, book shops, or sports equipment places); browsing around boats, cars, or airplanes or around sewing or food shops; or going to museums, nurseries, parks, or the zoo. When was the last time you browsed in a museum? In a park? Make a list of your interests, both past and present. For each interest, fill in the possible browse/wander Me-Acts you could do almost *any* day.

Another kind of Me-Act is best described as *puttering* or *messing about*. Joe putters in his basement workshop in the evenings. He makes wooden projects, puts things together, and tries things out. He does this alone, at his own pace. There's no rush and no pressure. He is not repairing things that break around the house or things that need to be fixed. This would set up a specific goal and, of course, would not be stress reducing. I ask Joe, "How do you feel about not finishing a project in an evening?" He answers, "It doesn't make any difference. Getting it done isn't that important; I just enjoy doing it." With this kind of an answer, Joe controls his mini-vacation and makes it a perfect Me-Act. Some people putter with hobbies or arts and crafts; others just putter around the house. Some people report that they can actually do housework as a Me-Act. No specific cleaning tasks that must be done, but a relaxing puttering around, arranging things, browsing through things and so on. Some people are able to putter in the garden—watering or weeding. No specific goal that says, "I have to get the lawn mowed this Saturday." That, again, would not be a Me-Act. "Messing about with boats," a familiar phrase from *The Wind in the Willows,* is a well-known Me-Act. List your puttering activities. Recall some old favorites from the past that might be reactivated again. Check out your list: Which of these could be done for thirty minutes after arriving home from work? Which at other times during the day? Which in the evenings? Don't restrict your Me-Acts only to weekends. As you do your self-monitoring, you probably will decide you do need a daily mini-vacation.

There are some other terms that describe Me-Acts that may also apply to you. *Play* is a term we usually apply to social activities, and it was discussed as such in Chapter 13. But play can also be solitary: One can play solitaire, play around with paints, play around in the sand with your big toe, or play with model trains or other hobbies. Playing around in the kitchen is a Me-Act, whereas cooking might be a stressful activity. The quality of goalless, aimless, simple waste of time is crucial to many of these Me-Acts.

There are two cautionary concerns that are important to consider as you plan your Me-Acts. These are concerns that can trip us up and reduce the stress release value considerably. First, goals, for some of us, are so important that they sneak in and ruin an otherwise good Me-Act. Work-a-holics are sorely tempted to turn relaxing activities into stressful ones. Art is the work-a-holic we mentioned in the Introduction, and he readily does just this sort of thing. Sometimes, on Saturday he's home alone; the family is out. Art has the house to himself, and his time is his own—a good opportunity for peace and quiet. He wants to relax. He sits for a bit, looks at the paper, and starts feeling restless. He gets up, starts pacing around the house, and suddenly he recalls that the lawn needs mowing and that it has to be done today. Before you know it, he's out there getting a specific job done. He's lost the opportunity for a Me-Act. Art restlessly seeks jobs to be done around the house, either for himself or for his family. He feels that aimless, meandering, puttering is a waste of time, and Art was trained very young not to waste time.

Working mothers and single parents often find themselves in this trap, too. They have so many responsibilities, so many tasks, and so many things to do that they often feel that there is no time to be aimless, to loaf, or to browse. They feel guilty taking the time to enjoy themselves. Unfortunately, even on rare vacations, these people often find themselves still working on specific needy goals. They do the cooking while camping out; they still have the kids to take care of. Their harried lives cry out for the goalless quality of a Me-Act, but they feel trapped with too many burdens.

The answer for Art, for working mothers, and for harassed single parents can be found by facing two issues. One: Recognize the need for self-care and renewal. The work-a-holic can sometimes buy the idea that the purpose of a Me-Act is to strengthen him- or herself. Then he or she can return more productively to his or her top priority, which, of course, is work. The primary purpose in "wasting" your lunch hour on renewal is to enable you to do a better job at work in the afternoon. For the working mother, taking time away from the family for a Me-Act would enable her to be a better mother and wife as well as a more loving, caring person. Me-Act serves the purpose of Re-Act. Work/family is still foremost, and the Me-Act supports that priority.

Secondly, many persons report that they also feel a great deal of guilt about taking time for relaxation when there is so much to be done. The issue of guilt is so crucial to dealing with stress that an entire chapter (Chapter 16) was devoted to it. Work-a-holics, working mothers, and all others where the shoe fits, take special note: perhaps you might turn back to Chapter 16 right now.

We can also lose some or all of our Me-Act value because of that old nasty influence again: competition!

John bowls for fun but not for stress release. He has a specific goal regarding the score he wants to get. If he doesn't get a high enough score, he is dissatisfied, he pushes himself harder, and he wants to work on bettering himself. Bowling, for John, is not a Me-Act. Joan, however, also bowls. But she does it for stress release. She would like to get a good score, but it is not that important. If she does badly, she shrugs her shoulders and says it was fun anyway. Bowling, for Joan, is a Me-Act. Her style is not competitive, even though bowling is a competitive sport.

If we adopt a competitive style, we can turn gardening, hobbies, crossword puzzles, or any other Me-Act into a Re-Act (see Figure 18–3). We do this by setting a specific self-competitive goal or expectation.

In Figure 18–3, we turn Me-Acts into Re-Acts by setting specific goals: I have to win a prize for my hobby; I want to swim faster than I did yesterday; I strive to walk as far as I can in my twenty minutes. This sets us up for dissatisfactions, disappointment, anger, and a host of other stressful emotions.

For those of you who are fairly competitive, turn to Chapter 20 on competition and stress. That chapter can help you to remain competitive where you have to be but show you how to avoid letting competition plague your entire life.

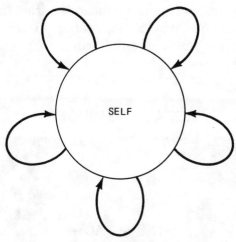

Setting Specific Goals
Figure 18–3

In summary, pull together your lists of wandering, browsing, loafing, messing about, puttering, and playing activities. Plan a specific time each day for a mini-vacation of the Me-Act type. Some days, you might not require this time; but most days, you will cherish it. Do this in addition to any other stress release activities of the more social type. Review Chapter 17 on solitude if necessary.

Remember that you must arrange your own Me-Acts. Rarely does someone at work or in your family tell you to take time off just to loaf. You, of course, must take responsibility for your own self-care.

Many individuals report that Me-Acts must actually be scheduled into their busy lives. Otherwise, that time is easily lost in the battle for precious time. Me-Act time must be defended valiantly against all temptations and all guilts. You will probably be most tempted to surrender your self-care time when things get tight and when time pressures are severe.

And yet, that is again the very time when we need our mini-vacations the most. "I'm too busy" really means "I don't realize I have to take care of myself and renew myself." This means, of course, my head is buried in the sand; I don't really know what's happening to me; I'm over-stressed! Review your self-monitoring!

RECALL REMINDER

18

THE ME-ACT

1. List all the Me-Acts you enjoy doing:

	When?	Past Me-Acts

2. Now go through your list and make a note in the "when" column about what time of day you could do the listed Me-Acts. Use the following abbreviations:

> L = Lunch hour.
> N = Things I can do at night.
> H = Things I can do at home.
> O = Outside Me-Acts.

3. In the last column, "Past Me-Acts," check some that you haven't done for a while and would like to reactivate in your life. When?

19
PHYSICAL HEALTH

When one considers the sheer quantity of popular writing in the fields of physical health and its allied concerns (nutrition, diet, and longevity), it would not surprise me if the informed reader felt thoroughly overwhelmed by it all. This chapter will add nothing specifically new to that barrage but will merely present three brief summaries for your consideration. If you feel unduly saturated by it all, move right on to the next chapter. I can empathize with you.

These three brief summaries offer only the basics, what is well founded and obvious. Why offer what is obvious? Simply because of our natural tendencies to lose sight of the trees while wandering through those overwhelming and perhaps frightening woods. The following, therefore, is mainly a review and reminder.

One of these obvious basics that has been given prior attention in this book is the intimate interconnection between stress (emotion) and physical health (body). Psyche-soma (mind/body) relations defy simple verbal labeling. The cliché again emphasizes an underlying truth: The mind and the body are one; stress and health are part of the

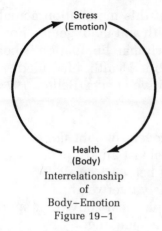

Interrelationship
of
Body–Emotion
Figure 19–1

same whole. Change in one results in change in the other (see Figure 19–1). This entire book deals with the upper part of Figure 19–1, the issue of the management of stress. What about the lower part of Figure 19–1, our physical health—the condition of our body?

The three brief summaries here deal with three separate parts of the lower (health) part of Figure 19—1. The choice has been made to include only generalized and accepted opinion. If your favored diet or approach is absent, it is not because I reject it or have a need to change your opinion. In the field of health, right now, we are in a state of change, of new concepts, and of inevitable confusion. The test of time and further scientific verification will undoubtedly tell us much more than we now know.

SUMMARY ONE: MODERATION

This old-fashioned word has become, in some quarters, the most frequently heard modern answer to the basic issues of health. It's okay to drink, but in moderation. Ditto for exercise or, for that matter, for anything else. Use common sense. Be reasonable.

The results of this moderation actually do pay off in good physical health and in longevity. For example, a study conducted by the Human Population Laboratory, California Department of Public Health, identified seven health practices that had positive effects (Belloc, 1973). These were as follows:

1. Sleeping seven to eight hours per day.
2. Eating breakfast almost every day.
3. Not eating between meals.
4. Not seriously overweight.
5. Moderate physical activity or sports.
6. No cigarette smoking.
7. Moderate alcohol consumption.

These seven good health habits dimly remind me of the health lessons I was taught way back in elementary school. Or perhaps you remember your old Boy or Girl Scout Handbook? However, these old-fashioned good health habits really work. The Department of Health has statistics to show that men who practice six to seven of these habits will live eleven years longer than men who practice only up to three of them. If eleven years of longer life doesn't seem significant to you, for comparison, look at the changes in life expectancy from 1900 to 1960. With all of modern medicine and its expensive technology, the life expectancy for adults (not children) since 1900 has only increased about three years, whereas these health habits alone result in an eleven-year increase!

SUMMARY TWO: THE BADDIES

Let's face some simple facts. The following are recognized culprits. They are harmful; they are not good for us. You know it; I know it. A list of the negative baddies we reach for when our stress level mounts follows:

Tobacco.
Alcohol.
Food.
Caffeine.
Sugar.
Tranquilizers.
Other Drugs.

If you are still hooked on some of them, you are certainly not alone. You belong to a large group of us (myself included). You can probably reduce your consumption to moderate (and healthy) levels by applying the stress management methods described in this book. This will work even if you are seriously dependent on these foods/drugs. Remember: The more moderate your stress level, the less often you reach for those negative baddies.

There are also courses, workshops, and organizations solely dedicated to helping you get unhooked. The major requirement seems to be a commitment on your part to give up your dependency (see Part Four on self-discipline). However, denial of potential harm will get you nowhere. Of the above, all are harmful. True, it may not get you. All smokers don't get lung cancer. Every smoker I meet knows an eighty-year-old man who smokes two packs a day. Statistically, there is such a man. They keep him locked up in a vault somewhere in Washington. If you smoke, go see him. But there is a chance that you won't live to be eighty if you smoke. Do you really want to take this chance?

SUMMARY THREE: REDUCING THE RISK OF HEART DISEASE

Heart disease is still the number one killer, increasingly so for younger persons and for women. It is well proven to be a cumulative disease. It probably begins at birth for most of us with cholesterol and other fats building up on the inside of our arteries. Studies from the Korean and Vietnamese Wars proved conclusively that 50 percent or more of American men aged thirty or younger already had marked arterial disease. These findings are attributed primarily to our fatty diet. The effects of stress on heart disease have been summarized in Chapter 1. Stress can be reduced, but so can other causative factors. Because the onset of heart disease is early and its development is slow, the time to reduce your risk of heart disease is now. See the chart in Figure 19–2 for

High blood pressure

High levels of cholesterol or other fatty substances in the blood

Overweight

Diabetes

Lack of exercise

Cigarette smoking

Reduce Your Risk of Heart Attack

Figure 19–2

risk factors (besides stress) that can be reduced, as summarized by the American Heart Association. All are obvious and achievable.

Just a few personal comments on exercise. It has not yet been conclusively proven that exercise can remove the fatty plaques that have accumulated on the inside of your arteries. However, special exercise called cardiovascular (or aerobic) exercise has a number of well-proven, healthy values for the heart. One summary statistic impresses me: If you exercise regularly and do get a heart attack, your chances of survival are three or four times better than someone who does not exercise.

That statistic is enough for me. My arteries are probably loaded with fat and cholesterol. Until six or seven years ago (when my father died of his third heart attack), I ate my share of ice cream, fatty meats, bacon and eggs, and all the rest. I am considerably older than thirty, and it would not surprise me if my clogged arteries (a coronary artery) gave up one day, and I had a heart attack. I am, however, relying on my daily walking, running, swimming, or cycling to save me. I put in thirty minutes to an hour, every day, on cardiovascular exercise. I am not a physical fitness bug. I am not an athlete, and I never have been one (I was always the last one chosen for the team in athletics). I do this for stress and heart disease prevention reasons. Remember, too, that if you do engage in cardiovascular exercise for heart disease prevention, you are also getting a great deal of regular LMA* activity, with all of its stress release value as well. All you Mark Twains, here's another reason to get that body moving!

---

* Note carefully that all the muscle activities listed in the LMA chapter (Chapter 7) are not cardiovascular. For an exercise to be cardiovascular (or aerobic), you must exercise regularly, at least three times per week, for thirty minutes to one hour. The exercise must be rhythmic and continuous, no stopping or time out (see references).

RECALL REMINDER

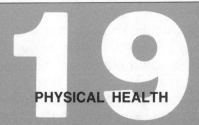

PHYSICAL HEALTH

I could become more moderate in the following habits that affect my body:

I want to reduce my use of the following baddies:

I will reduce my heart attack risk by changing the following:

THE COMPETITIVE CHALLENGE

I bicycle a great deal. I bicycle for fun and exercise, for relaxation, and for stress release. I began my adult career as a bicyclist a number of years ago. During those earlier adult bicycling times, I usually found biking a real stress release. I'd pump down the road at my own pace, comfortably and enjoyably. This went on, however, only until I saw another bicyclist. Then immediately my old competitive nature came to the fore. Dr. Jekyll emerged, and I engaged in sinful competitive thoughts. "Is he going faster than me?" "Can I beat him?" This instantly blew the relaxed, stress-releasing nature of my biking. Being competitive, too, was also embarrassing: Young kids and even older ladies would shoot right by me. Giving in to these competitive urges completely ruined what could have been a stress-releasing Me-Act type of activity for me.

I am competitive. Probably many of you reading this book are, too. You probably wouldn't be in the work you are in or in the position you are in if you didn't have at least some competitive strivings.

Our competitive drives can cause us a great deal of stress. Competition and stress go hand in hand. Let's take a look at four ways that competition can affect our stress levels.

THE COMPETITIVE CHALLENGE

Many of us recognize our competitive drives as a pretty basic part of ourselves—built right in, part of our very guts, as it were. We see the rest of the world as potential competitors, as persons to beat. We have to perform better and be more successful. We have to win, to be promoted, to receive job awards and successes, and to gain a variety of status indicators. This affects us on the job but also spills over into our recreation, our sports, our games (cards, for example), and our hobbies (we have to win prizes). In perhaps slightly milder form, the competitive challenge means we have to possess the best, the newest, the most prestigious, the highest quality, or the biggest. This means the very best car, stereo equipment, or house. Or this means the best in recreation, the "in" thing, the newest—whether in equipment, sports clothes, or the place to go on vacation. If you want clear-cut evidence of the power of this competition, listen carefully to the wording of TV commercials or other advertising and notice, however subtly, how competition is emphasized as an appeal.

Many of us also engage directly in competitive sports: We keep score, we have to win or to do better next time. Sailboat racing, golf, bowling, racquetball, bicycle racing, or singles tennis—you name it. The more competitive the drive, the more we have to win. For some of us, the need to win is not as important as is the need not to lose. What is most painful seems to be facing failure (see Chapter 8 on the Do-nut). The stronger these feelings, the higher the stress. Losing or fear of losing are probably the ultimate emotions that drive us.

SELF-COMPETITION

Some of us avoid social competition but engage in competition with ourselves. We keep score on ourselves; we set standards and goals for ourselves. We push ourselves just as hard, perhaps harder, when we compete with ourselves. We are not satisfied with where we are now; we always have to do better. The standards, goals, and scores are always higher or better. These push us, propel us, or drive us in our activities. We can self-compete at work as well as in any area of our lives. If it spills over into non-job activities, it can add considerably to our job stress. When we leave work, we get no relief from competitive pressures.

SNEAKY COMPETITION

After I recognized that my biking for stress release was going down the tubes because of my competitive drive to beat others (or not to be beaten), I was able to rid myself of it. I did this by becoming aware of its stressful effect. I could then control it and not let it bother me. But then I found that competition (in me) can be sneaky. If I saw another bicycle, I stopped chasing it but found myself wondering what kind of bike it was, how expensive it was, what kind of derailleur it had, or how new or fancy its equipment was. This also blew the stress release value of biking.

How important is it for you to go to the best restaurant, for your son to get high (the highest) grades, or for you to be the funniest or the social center of attention? Do you find yourself convincing others how wonderful you are or how many high prestige meetings you attend? Do you name-drop or brag about the number of keys you have to your "executive washroom?" Remember: You are not going to be obvious about this. You're just going to sneak it in sideways. Be honest. This can be a powerful motivation. Sneaky competition reflects a more underlying competition, somewhat disguised. It can, however, increase our stress in areas of our lives where it is not really necessary to be stressful. It can prevent us from relaxing, letting our hair down, trying to develop closeness, or having fun. Instead, we are still competing.

JOB COMPETITION

In many of our jobs, the element of competition is very real. Some of us do need to compete with others for customers, for clients, or for patients. Some of us do need to compete with many others just to obtain a job, to get a promotion, or for an opening in a special school or training program. We feel the need to get the boss' attention in the right way to get ahead; we need to do better than our coworkers or to stand out in some special way.

This work competition can set the pace for our work day and can keep us at a high level of competitiveness (and consequently, stress) all day long. The anxiety, concern, and fear associated with competition can plague us in varying degress. If things are likely to go badly, the anxiety can add powerfully to our stress and is likely to affect our feelings, our behavior, and our bodies. If things do go badly—if we lose a client, get a bad evaluation or a criticism, get passed over for a promotion, or lose our jobs—our stress level inevitably mounts, and our reactions can become even more extreme.* Self-monitoring here is crucial in order to determine when, if necessary, steps must be taken to manage that stress and to lower it.

What are the steps to be taken to minimize the harmful effects of competition?

1. First, because of our competitive natures, many of us see competition when it's not really there. Either that or we put more competition in the job situation than is necessary. Too much competition in work can actually result in reduced efficiency, in too much energy wasted in worry, fear, and dissatisfaction. It can increase squabbles of all kinds, lower teamwork and cohesiveness, and reduce morale. To get a job done requires cooperation, working together. The negative effects of too much competition are coun-

---

*Research sponsored by the National Institute of Occupational Safety and Health showed that workers facing a plant shutdown had increases in ulcers, high blood pressure, and swollen joints, as well as speeded up arterial clogging.

terproductive. Many of us interpret human survival as "survival of the fittest" and apply this to our own job situations.†

How much competition is actually required in your work? How much is clearly lowering your job effectiveness? What would you actually lose by fostering noncompetitive attitudes in yourself, such as loyalty, cooperation, companionship, and affection? What might you and your job gain by such attitudes? Answer honestly, please!

2. Recognize that if your work must be competitive, there is real value in eliminating competition from all other areas of your life. Noncompetitive activity can be truly relaxing, renewing, and recharging. Noncompetitive activity can be stress lowering and can make you more reasonable, rational, and sensible. Noncompetitive activity can strengthen you to return to face the struggle, the battle, the losses, and the hurts.

Consider, then, eliminating competition from your family life, your recreation, your play, your friendships, and your relations with men and with women.

3. If competitive sports are important to you and you don't want to give them up, do you also want to use them for *stress release*? You can use competitive sports for stress lowering, depending on your attitude. The test is simple. If you lose, score badly, or perform poorly, check out your reaction by self-monitoring. How do you feel afterwards? If you can truly say, "I tried the best I could; I enjoyed it; it's okay; I don't mind," then you pass the test. Check out your behavior and your body, too. Remember that our bodies do not respond well to competition.**

---

†Actually, modern biology emphasizes the *opposite* kinds of life values—symbiotic relationships, interdependence, and cooperation. Read, for example, *The Lives of a Cell* (Thomas, 1975).

**Competitiveness is one of the traits of the Type A or heart attack-prone personality (see Rosenman & Friedman, 1974). Also, competitive athletes do sometimes die of heart attacks. For a lengthy discussion of how much of this may be caused by excessive competitive drive, see Higdon, 1977: Chapter 7, Death of a Distance Runner.

Remember, too, that athletes are more successful when relaxed, not when highly stressed. Too much tension in sports lowers coordination and accuracy. Doesn't it do that for you?

4. If you would like to eliminate competitive sports from your recreation but would like to retain fun, excitement, socializing, and so on, you have many alternatives. Consider possibilities described in other chapters, such as large muscle activity (how about dancing, running, or jumping rope?); play (and other pleasurable goodies); and even the quieter, tender things like the Me-Act. If you want hearty, vigorous, skillful physical activity without competition, look into the New Games. These are cooperative games that have been developed to offer challenge, excitement, and fun without anyone losing or getting hurt. They can be played by children, families, or adults. Colleges and universities are beginning to adapt or develop New Games to replace the old-fashioned competitive intramural activities. These games are creative, sometimes wild, and crazy but are always fun. Can you imagine pitching to your own team, having an underwater jacks tournament, or determining the winners in a basketball tournament by the collective scores of both opponents? (Orlick, 1978).

Our family rather unintentionally invented a New Game several years ago. We call it Goodminton (badminton would be immoral, right?), In Goodminton, the object of play is to keep the birdie up in the air as long as possible. You try to hit it to your opponent in such a fashion that he or she can hit it back to you. If you blow it and hit it badly so that your opponent misses, naturally you would apologize.

Check out the reference to Orlick's work (1978); you may find the New Games exhilarating, stress lowering, and fun.

5. Watch the sneaky part of competition. In order to retain the stress-lowering nature of your biking, running, golf, and so on, you must eliminate sneaky competition, and it can be done. By being aware of it, you can stop it from affecting you. Of course, those of us who are highly competitive may have to be forever vigilant (sort of like being an alcoholic, isn't it?), but you can enjoy sports and physical activity without losing the stress-lowering value. Recognize what it's doing to you!

6. Search out in your life the noncompetitive reasons for your behavior. What activities do you engage in not to win, or to gain a reward, or for external approval? You may be surprised at how much of your own behavior is motivated by the following:

> Doing what is morally right, good, proper, or appropriate.
>
> Doing something because you like, love, admire, or respect someone.
>
> Doing something because you are modeling a person you admire or respect.
>
> Doing something only because it interests, excites, stimulates or inspires you (turns you on).
>
> Doing something out of a feeling of pride in teamwork, cooperation, group belonging, or loyalty.
>
> Doing something just for a personal sense of achievement.
>
> Doing what is healthy.
>
> Doing something for fun.
>
> Doing something because of a self-imposed sense of duty or ethics.

Much more of our behavior than we are aware of is not competitive. It is based on reasons such as those above. Discuss this question with your spouse or partner and with your coworkers or colleagues. See how large a list you come up with!

RECALL REMINDER

THE COMPETITIVE CHALLENGE

I would like to become less competitive in my recreation activities. Which ones:

I would gain more by becoming less competitive with the following people at work:

I have to watch out for sneaky competition while doing the following:

21

SEX

This chapter title is almost pure deception. I simply wanted to attract your attention. I would like you to consider again the possibility of moving your muscles for stress lowering (routine LMA), using whatever technique you prefer—sex included. For you readers who are persistent Mark Twains (and I know that many of you are), you may already have forgotten (or did you ignore) the LMA chapter (Chapter 7). Many of you have withdrawn considerably from physical activity. Even our middle-class vocabulary reflects how far we have come from the caveman (frontiersman, farmer, laborer) level of physical activity. Words that in the past actually described physical action are now used to mean typical, nonphysical, office activities. In the office we beat, jog, jump, climb, and so on (see Figure 21—1), and none of it is actually movement of muscles, nor does it relieve any stress! Since this is a chapter on sex, I should add to this list "chasing the boys or girls." Some of you, perhaps, are thinking of moving your muscles more regularly. I do realize that thinking about muscle movement may be the first step in actually getting to moving those muscles. Perhaps this chapter will encourage you to take the next step.

LMA was discussed in Part Two on stress lowering, but it is being discussed here as well under self-care. Moving one's muscles regularly is a necessity for caring for one's body. The body was made to move: Activity is our normal state. Move your body. Move it if you are tense, restless; you feel hungry, if you want a cigarette, or if you've been sitting too long. Note the effect on your emotions, your mood, and your stress.

Here's another illustration of some of the effects of regular LMA. One manager applied LMA not only to herself but to her office staff. Instead of taking two breaks during the day (morning and afternoon), she talked her staff into going for a walk instead. Their building was on a slight hill, and the office staff as a group spent their two breaks walking up and down the hill. The results were less squabbling in the office, less irritability, and an average weight loss of seven to twelve pounds (they gave up rolls and coffee in order to walk). Give this one a try!

Figure 21–1

Burn Off Pounds In Your Office

A recent report by the Southern California Medical Association pointed out that proper weight control and physical fitness cannot be attained by dieting alone. A particular problem is faced by the manager who spends most of his or her day behind a desk. Too many of these people fail to realize that calories can be burned off by the hundreds by engaging in strenuous exercises that are common for office workers.

The following list of calorie-burning activities is followed by the number of calories per hour that may be used:

Beating around the bush	75
Jogging your memory	125
Jumping to conclusions	100
Climbing the walls	150
Swallowing your pride	50
Passing the buck	25
Grasping at straws	75
Beating your own drum	100
Throwing your weight around	50–300
(depending on weight)	
Dragging your heels	100
Pushing your luck	250
Making mountains out of molehills	500
Hitting the nail on the head	50
Spinning your wheels	175
Flying off the handle	225
Turning the other cheek	75
Wading through paperwork	300
Bending over backwards	75
Jumping on the bandwagon	200
Balancing the books	23
Beating your head against the wall	150
Patting yourself on the back	25
Sticking your neck out	175
Racing against time	300
Running around in circles	100
Chewing nails	200
Eating crow	225
Fishing for compliments	50
Tooting your own horn	25
Climbing the ladder of success	750
Pulling out the stoppers	75
Adding fuel to the fire	150
Pouring salt on the wound	50
Wrapping it all up at day's end	12

Courtesy of the Postal Inspector's Newsletter

Do you need LMA if you are already getting plenty of exercise during your paid work time? Generally, our work activity, because it is work, carries stress with it. Even though our muscles are moving, our stress is often being raised by the tense nature of the work. Stewardesses (who walk a great deal in their work) and nurses (who also walk) find routine LMA (such as running or swimming) exceptionally valuable for stress release. Custodians have also found LMA helpful. If you use your muscles at work, you still want to choose a routine LMA that is enjoyable. You may want, too, to choose an LMA that uses different muscles than your job does. Obviously, the above-mentioned stewardesses and nurses who ran for their LMA did not choose to exercise different muscles.

If, at this point in the book, you are beginning to seriously consider beginning routine LMA, there are several cautions.

First, the necessity for the traditional medical exam.* The most persistent diagnostic recommendation I hear is for a treadmill stress test (for all persons over thirty-five years of age). This test assesses your heart action while under physical stress. A cardiologist is present in the room (it's serious). I understand that this test is much more useful for assessing cardiovascular condition that the type of EKG we take lying down horizontally on a table. Some companies pay for their management to have treadmill stress tests. It might well be worth your while.

Second, if you have any of those hurried, rushed, competitive traits mentioned as comprising the heart attack-prone, Type A personality, you will have trouble engaging in LMA properly. You will want to start out big, move fast,

---

* Some physical fitness specialists and M. D.s are beginning to de-emphasize traditional medical exams. They don't always pay off in diagnosing potential problems. See, for example, Higdon (1977).

and do as much as you can. Nix. What is required is a small start (maybe walking only a few blocks) and a slow increase in small increments (add a few blocks at a time). This will be difficult for some of you. Pushing in your typical hurried, competitive fashion might have two possible results: You could have a heart attack, or you could so successfully overdo it that you would ache and hurt so much afterwards that you'd give up on physical exercise altogether. Either result is an effective cop-out: LMA isn't for me.

Now, to return to sex. Sex activity is on the list as one of the possible large muscle activities. Sometimes, the reaction I get to this is, "It's not a large muscle activity, only a small one." However you view it, sex can be an important means of relieving stress. And it can become a form of large muscle activity. Extending your sexual involvement to include more of your body, through extensive touching and foreplay, often enriches the experience considerably. The more your entire body becomes involved in making love, the more satisfying it is, and the more the release. Most of us, after a positive sexual experience, feel a sense of peace, a calmness, and a loss of stress, and we may also have a new and better perspective on things. You probably wouldn't want to engage in love making when angry (try another technique first in order to lower your emotion) or when you feel distant (try venting first in order to develop closeness). Otherwise, engage in sexual love in order to feel close, to feel support, to feel love—all neat feelings to have when under stress. Even masturbation relieves some physical tension.

I once had a member of a large audience come up to me after a talk where I mentioned sex and LMA. I had just defined regular LMA as being activity engaged in six to seven times per week for thirty minutes to an hour each time. He simply asked, "Give me a note for my wife, will ya, Doc?" What a goal to work towards!

RECALL REMINDER

21
SEX

What regular, routine LMA will I actually, really, honestly begin soon?

How can I develop more closeness and release while making love? I would like to discuss this with my partner or spouse.

IV

CAN I REALLY CHANGE?

22
PERSONAL STRENGTHS

In times of high stress, many persons report that they lose sight of their positive qualities. At those times, we aren't cognizant of our abilities and talents; we don't recall past successes and accomplishments. We may indulge in a downer or a bout of self-dislike, or we may even feel anger toward ourselves.

There are some specific things we can do during these high stress periods to bolster up our falling egos or to put us more in contact with what is positive about ourselves. These techniques put our total job and other accomplishments in a more realistic perspective. They can truly bolster us during stressful periods.

POSITIVE COMMENDATION FILE

At a time of lowered stress, collect all the written citations, commendations, testimonials, references, and so on that you have in your files. Collect, too, the awards, certificates, and diplomas you have attained. All these items can be used by you later during times of stress. Some people store all these in one desk drawer or in a file. Then, when things get tough, they open the drawer or file, pull each item out one by one, and slowly read it—perhaps even relish or savor it, item by item.

Another use of this laudatory material was suggested by a manager who frequently deals with angry, attacking taxpayers (clients, customers, etc.). He collected all these items and had them framed. He then placed them on the wall where he could see them by just looking up from his desk. As the angry taxpayer (client, etc.) faced him and told him what a rotten job he was doing and how inefficient his department was, he could merely raise his eyes slightly over the person's head to see an entire wall framed with "goodies" about himself. Very uplifting!

POSITIVE TRAIT LIST

Acquiring a list of goodies that others have said about you is nice, but another source of positive feelings comes from within ourselves. Have you ever sat down and listed your own positive traits, your abilities, your strengths, and your personal qualities? Consider taking the time to do this, again at a period of lowered stress. Don't forget to include your personal qualities—for example, "I have a good sense of humor," or "I am a resourceful person," or "I am sensitive to others feelings." Just making this list of your own strengths is typically experienced as a positive high.

If you haven't made such a list before, you may be uncomfortable doing it the first time. Many of us were taught, "It's not nice to praise yourself" or "Don't boost yourself." However, you are not doing this to feel superior but solely to obtain an accurate view of how you see yourself. It might help to start with those external commendations from others. But then move on and list all those positive qualities you see in yourself. One good time to do this is before your supervisor sits down with you for your next job evaluation.

If you did feel uncomfortable making this list the first time, the more often you do it, the less difficult it becomes.

The more often you do it, too, you will discover more new positive qualities as well as being reminded of all the old ones. Save your list; don't lose it. You may want to pull it out during times of stress to help you gain perspective on yourself.

This list of your positive qualities may help you to feel less negative about your job, your boss, a client, or a customer. It works that way because the better we feel about ourselves, the better we feel about the outside world.

Remember those days when you wake up, the sun is shining, you feel great, and everything seems to be wonderful, when you're glad to be alive? (Now, you do remember at least one of those days, don't you?) On those days, things that people say or do rarely bother you. Yet on a day when you already feel negative about yourself, those very same things that people say or do may drive you up a wall. If someone just breathes the wrong way, it pushes you right up the emotional temperature chart. The more positive you feel about yourself, the less likely it is that job stressors are going to push your high stress buttons. Add your own positive trait list to your external commendation file, and you now have a double list of goodies.

BECOME LESS DEPENDENT ON THE APPROVAL OR DISAPPROVAL OF OTHERS

We don't need to depend heavily on others to tell us if we have done a good job or performed well. It is true that generally we tend to evaluate our job success by the following external criteria: What does the boss/superior say? What do the statistics report about my performance? It is certainly necessary that we relate to the external criteria in order to survive in our work. However, almost everyone who has been in a job for any length of time or is dedicated to a career develops his or her own criteria for job performance. These criteria include the external standards but are also independent of them. Our self-determined standards arise out of our own personal experience in actually doing the work and out of our specialized knowledge of the job. These standards also depend on our own interpretations of the work in terms of our unique intelligence and our special abilities. Someone else in the same job might do it differently, might even do different things.

Since we all do have our own criteria, we might put more confidence in them and trust them more. To be too dependent on external approval can weaken us. Every time the stats drop, we drop. Every time the boss has a fight with his wife and is critical, we are crushed. We want to become less dependent on these external criteria for our own emotional temperature.

Spend some time clarifying for yourself your own criteria for your job performance. Articulate these; perhaps write them down. What is it that you have best to give to your job? What are your special interests and your unique job talents? Add your criteria to your boss' criteria.

Have faith in your criteria. Become less dependent on the ups and downs of the outside world. Most of the time, your criteria will be valid, meaningful, and significant.*

OTHER SOURCES OF PERSONAL STRENGTH

Personal strength in coping with job stress may originate in activities that have nothing to do with our work activity. A very good illustration of this is the concept of Positive Addiction developed by Glasser (Glasser, 1976). Glasser discovered that engaging routinely for many months, about an hour every day, in the same activity and doing this in a noncritical and noncompetitive fashion can result in a source of personal strength he labels a "Positive Addiction"

* Am I crazy or is the rest of the world crazy? Be careful how you answer this: They might lock you up. Actually, both external and internal criteria have to be valid, or you won't be happy in your job, and your boss won't be happy with you.

state. He calls these addictions because basically we feel withdrawal symptoms if we miss doing them for a day or two. The kind of activity is not important. It can be running or biking, but it also can be meditation or playing the organ, knitting or grooming oneself. The important result is that we gain in inner strength, in self-discipline. People attribute this personality gain to participation in the activity: "I wouldn't have gotten through my divorce if it wasn't for my daily exercise program," or "My personal therapy is playing the piano every day." From *Positive Addiction* by William Glasser, the criteria for achieving a Positive Addiction state are the following:

1. It is something noncompetitive that you choose to do, and you can devote an hour (approximately) a day to it.
2. It is possible for you to do it easily, and it doesn't take a great deal of mental effort for you to do it well.
3. You can do it alone or rarely with others, but it does not depend upon others to do it.
4. You believe that it has some value (physical, mental, or spiritual) for you.
5. You believe that if you persist at it you will improve, but this is completely subjective—you need to be the only one who measures that improvement.
6. The activity must have the quality that you can do it *without criticizing yourself. If you can't accept yourself during this time, the activity will not be addicting.*

You might want to check this one out for yourself. It could be a useful and fascinating concept for you. If you have to be addicted to something, why not choose an addiction that fosters personal strength instead of those negative, harmful ones?

GROWING, LEARNING, RENEWING, AND FLEXIBILITY

The last source of inner strength that can be of great help in terms of stress has to do with our growing and learning potential. We are all capable of learning new ways or giving up old ways and of growing and stretching our minds; we are capable of flexibility, rather than the same old, rigid, solutions to life's problems.

We may need to encourage and nurture this growing, learning part of ourselves. It may be too easy and comfortable to keep viewing our job situations in the same old ways. We get caught in a perceptual rut and seem to dig our wheels deeper and deeper into the same old mental groove. There are alternatives; there are possibilities. You don't have to do it that way or any single way. You have learned new things in your life, and you can learn again. No matter how well it worked in the past, it might not work now. Consider the following:

> All the adjustments you have made in your life.
> All the changes you have dealt with.
> All the crises you have been through.
> The new solutions you have evolved to your life problems.

You've done it before; you can do it again. Perhaps you'd like some further help in starting to move again when undergoing crises and stresses. A list of suggestive starters follows:

> Listen to someone who is excited about what he or she is doing; excitement is contagious.
> Take a course, attend a lecture, read a book, and so on—in something new or something you've always wanted to do.

Make a new friend.

Discover a new way to earn money.

Seek out something positive, interesting, or loving in someone at work whom you just can't stand.

At work, find a new way to do an old thing.

Sincerely try to understand your boss' feelings.

Learn to cook, or garden, or tune the engine in your car.

Try using a bicycle to go to and from work.

Travel to a new place.

Do something you've always been afraid of doing.

Dream, fantasize, or brainstorm.

Eat a new food or some old foods in new combinations.

Add your own!_____

And last, but far from least, watch the unfolding of new leaves in early spring. Listen to the songs of birds mating. Look for the small bud that blooms into the spectacular flower. Recall how the earth and all the living things in it are eternally involved in renewal and rebirth. You, too, are a part of this.

Don't lose sight of your strengths. You have a lot going for you!

RECALL REMINDER

PERSONAL STRENGTHS

Check suggestions I would like to try:

_____I might find it useful to collect all my certificates, diplomas, letters, and so on.

_____I would like to try sitting down by myself and developing my own "positive qualities" list.

_____I will develop further my own criteria for my job performance.

_____I'd like to check into the concept of Positive Addictions. When?

_____I'd like to try to develop flexibility, renewing, and learning. How?

23
STOP INDULGING YOUR FEELINGS

I bicycle a great deal. There are days, however, when I get on my bicycle, wheel down the driveway, head down the street, and it just doesn't feel good. It's cold or windy; those old muscles of mine feel stiff or achy; I just don't feel like bicycling. On those days, if I listened too intently to those feelings, I would just take that bicycle, turn it around, and head right back into the garage. I'd give in to my feelings, because it just didn't feel right.

I rarely do that. I usually keep pedaling because my head tells me what my feelings don't tell me: I will feel better after a while; my muscles will loosen up and stop aching. I will get warm (so warm I have to take off my jacket); it will feel great. I know, too, that bicycling is the right thing to do, both for stress release and cardiovascular fitness. I am also aware of my commitment to regular LMA. As a consequence of what my mind tells me, I don't indulge my feelings. But believe me, there are some mornings when I am sorely tempted!

There are lots of times we give in to our feelings or are tempted to. Not just regarding our commitments to eat less, to give up cigarettes, to stop biting our nails, or to have one less drink but also in the stress area of our lives. We don't stick to our commitments to take better care of ourselves, to take time for self-renewal, or to stop running so fast and so hard. We also make commitments not to feel so dissatisfied, angry, or worried about work; not to feel fear, inadequacy, or anger in the face of the boss or other authority; not to resort to ingrained, less satisfactory methods of stress relief. In all these commitments, our self-discipline can be shaky indeed. Our immediate, spontaneous feelings may very well run counter to our serious, dedicated, committed goals. And often (or check the appropriate answer: sometimes_____; occasionally_____), we give in to those feelings; we indulge them.

Let's take a look at some of the factors that seem to affect us in indulging feelings. Understanding some of these might help us at times to resist the temptation and to remain committed to our values and ideals.

CULTURAL SUPPORT

For some years now in American society, there has been much support for indulging feelings. It's been a big cultural thing: Do what you feel like doing; do your own thing; do what feels good. Psychologists in the past (including, I must confess, myself), have encouraged this. Lots of cultural support still exists. Possibly we've gone too far. It seems like another case of the old swinging pendulum (see Figure 23–1). As I look at my own family background, the swing has been fairly rapid. My grandparents (Jewish, Russian) did not marry whom they felt like marrying (remember *Fiddler on the Roof?*). Their marriage was arranged on the basis of duty and responsibility. Sometimes it's hard for me to believe it, but that was the order of things. It wasn't really that long ago that sweeping cultural changes occurred regarding tradition (remember the song, "Tradition," from *Fiddler?*), duty, loyalty, and honor. In *Fiddler*, of course, the change took place with Tevye's five daughters, all of

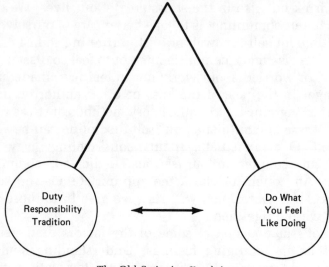

The Old Swinging Pendulum
Figure 23–1

whom did the radical thing of marrying on the basis of their feelings.

Not all of us are heavily into the "do your own thing" life style, but almost all of us have been influenced by it, at least to some extent. Look at the pendulum for yourself. Where are you right now in your life—more oriented toward tradition and duty or toward "doing what you feel like doing?" Which way is it swinging for you? Which way do you want it to go?

HEAVY RESPONSIBILITY

For some of us, the issue is one of feeling too heavily the stresses of duty and responsibility. Our jobs (and/or families) weigh us down with the burden of duties, tasks, and responsibilities (see Figure 23–2). In the process, it seems like we are being neglected: We don't give enough weight to ourselves; we consider ourselves too lightly. In this kind of

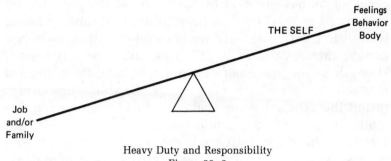

Heavy Duty and Responsibility
Figure 23–2

burdened life situation, we often want to indulge our feelings. We want to do what we feel like doing and not always
do what we *have* to do.

Where in our lives can we let loose, indulge ourselves,
and do what we feel like doing? Generally, not on the job.
Most people remain severely dedicated and conscientious
in their work. What about doing what we feel like doing in
the family arena of our lives? Most of us may be willing to
indulge some feelings here (perhaps transfer some stress/
anger to our family), but in general, we maintain our responsibilities. It looks as if the only place to let go and to do
our own thing is with reference to our personal selves: our
feelings, our behaviors, and our bodies. And many of us do
just that. We give in to our feelings: We eat, smoke, and
drink more; we indulge our anger or depression or our lazy,
escapist feelings; or we neglect healthy habits and the like.

Does your self-discipline break down more readily
after a stressful day or week at work? Do you feel that you
are entitled to that extra plate of ice cream or that third
drink because you've had such a hard day? Do you blast (in
fantasy or words) your boss or a customer because rules,
regulations, or immutable work changes have become
worse? Do you say, "The hell with it" or "I don't give a
damn" in your personal life because that's the one place
you *can* say it?

WHY DISCIPLINE OURSELVES?

Some of us have tended in our personal lives to give up behaving the way duty, responsibility, tradition, or honor tells us to behave. Because we have rejected these behavior codes/guides, we have to fall back rather heavily on the strength of our own self-discipline. What's the source of that self-discipline? For many of us, discipline has always meant the externally imposed—the rules, regulations, dictates, or laws of an outside authority—our parents, our teachers, the organization or company we work for, our bosses, the state legislature, and so on. Our control or discipline of ourselves has been primarily in order to avoid punishment imposed by that external authority or to get those external goodies handed out by that authority: for example, promotions, high grades, or a pat on the back.

In situations where no immediate punishment or reward seems imminent, we may not feel anywhere near as motivated to control ourselves. If I won't catch it, I can ignore it and do what I feel like doing. So, if we are convinced that no harm will come to us from mistreating our bodies, from acting badly, or from doing what is not right, we may go right ahead and do it. "I'm not going to die of lung cancer"; "My marriage won't fall apart"; "My secretary understands if I blast her once in a while": All indicate that we expect no immediate punishment for behaving badly or expect no great reward for behaving properly.

There are, however, many significant reasons for behaving properly and for doing the right thing. These valid reasons have nothing to do with avoiding someone's disapproval or attempting to gain the carrot held out for us. These motivations lack a label, but they are generally considered inner-directed rather than externally compelling. For example, when driving a car, why do you stop at a stop sign? Is it merely to avoid the risk of a ticket? What if there is no policeman obviously present? Why, then, do you stop? There are other reasons for doing the right thing besides fear of punishment or seeking a reward. In your job situation, or family, consider the following:

> What do you do because you care about people?
> What do you do because it's the right, ethical thing to do?
> What do you do because it's the best way or the good way?
> What do you do because of an agreement or a commitment that is sacred to you?
> What do you do for someone because you admire or respect him or her?
> What do you do because it is healthy and good?
> (Check out Chapter 20 on competition and stress for a larger list.)

Check out your own self: Where on the scale would you put yourself (see Figure 23–3)? If you feel that you are too oriented toward the external, look for more self-imposed reasons for your behaviors. Look at your own beliefs, values, and traditions, or look at the people you admire, respect, and love. Where would you rate yourself; which motivations are really more important to you? In your work situation? In your family? In your personal self-care? What kind of an employee do you truly want to be? What kind of father or mother? Husband or wife? These are your answers, no one else's.

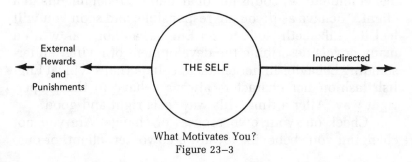

What Motivates You?
Figure 23–3

FEELINGS FIRST OR BEHAVIOR FIRST?

Some of the rationale for the "indulge your feelings" emphasis is based on a psychotherapeutic principle that is sometimes stated like this: "Understand and accept your feelings—only then will your behavior modify or change." Simply put, in order to change, we must change our feelings first; then our behavior will change to be consistent with our feelings. In psychotherapy, the alcoholic or depressed client must first accept (face) his feelings, and then he will behave more constructively and healthily.

Sound though this may be, the opposite aproach is also therapeutic: "Change your behavior first; then new feelings will develop consistent with your new behavior." Recall *Fiddler*. After twenty-five years of an arranged marriage, Tevye asks, in his song to his wife, "Do you love me?", and her beautifully poignant answer is, "Do I what? After twenty-five years. . . ."

The psychological theory underlying racial integration is similar: integrating the races in order to change negative prejudice (feelings) by first establishing integration behavior (bringing the two races together). The result of this behavior change is more positive feelings of one race toward the other (and many studies have verified this). This happens, of course, only when certain behavior conditions are met, but the basic theory is solidly based on research: Changed behavior can cause changes in feelings. Behavior first; feelings follow. Other examples: A singing teacher tells her students, "Act as if you are confident and you will feel confident." A counselor of alcoholics recommends to a client, "Behave as if you are responsible, and soon you will feel it." Elizabeth Goudge, an English author, has written many novels describing the development of loving, understanding behavior in her characters. In perhaps typical English fashion her characters always behave in the proper, right way. After a time, this way feels right and good.

Check out your own process of change. Are you not changing your behavior toward a coworker, client, or customer (or the boss) because you are awaiting a radical change in your feelings? Are you relying on positive feelings to sustain you in your job or on loving feelings to sustain your marriage or your relationship with your children? Are you discovering that your feelings are not always positive and loving? Your feelings cannot always be positive, friendly, and loving. You might try developing friendly, positive, and loving behavior (because it is the right way to behave), and then see if your feelings will follow suit. Don't always wait for your feelings to guide you.

In summary, now, are you indulging your feelings too much? Have you discovered that your immediate feelings aren't always that great? Perhaps you need to use your mind more to tell you what is right, what is proper, and what is healthy. Don't always let your feelings direct you; you have other guides as well. Your intellect, your brain, and your mind can powerfully serve in helping you discipline yourself toward becoming the kind of person you want to be.

RECALL REMINDER

**STOP INDULGING
YOUR FEELINGS**

List the feelings I want to indulge less or give in to less often:

Which inner-directed motivations do I want to develop more in my work and in my total life (see page 219, page 195)

A CODE
OF BEHAVIOR

We all have some code or ideal that we use to help guide our behavior in times of stress. We acquire these codes from a number of sources. Many times we are strongly influenced in our choice of ideals by the super-ideals and super-persons offered us by the mass media of our society.

Society pressures encourage us to emulate people who keep their stress/anger inside, hide it, or cover it up. The kind of persons (super-persons) we admire and try to model ourselves after are typically people who always appear "cool," act calm, appear to be well in control of themselves, and rarely if ever show extremes of emotion or stress. The "successful executive," the "Jacqueline Kennedy" wife, the "smart sophisticate," the "all-powerful male," and the "mature adult" are images that exist in our society and therefore in our minds as well.

Let's take a look at some of these images and ideals and see if any of them apply to your own handling of stress.

Do you find yourself trying to act like the "mature" and "successful" or "competent" employee who behaves in the following ways:

Gets along well with others (doesn't rock the boat).

Doesn't ever have any problems (that interfere with his or her work).

Doesn't ever appear flustered (that's a weak, feminine trait).

Doesn't show stress/emotion (not at work).

Doesn't show the outside world any vulnerability (the tower of strength).

Doesn't get angry or dissatisfied (only immature people do that).

Can't be hurt by others (too strong for that).

Never needs others (well, hardly ever).

Is self-sufficient.

Bears his or her burdens well (carries them on his or her shoulders).

Never needs to bother other people with his or her problems (obviously a weakness).

If, in addition, you are living up to the managerial or professional ideal, besides all of the above, you are probably trying to act as if:

You are always confident, sure, and in control of things.

You don't ever feel lonely, isolated, or separate from your subordinates, spouse, or others.

You know how to cope competently with all situations and how to handle all problems.

You don't have too close feelings for subordinates.

You are the "strong one"; other people come to you with their problems.

Which of the above fit you? Make a mental note of them for yourself, or use the Recall Reminder list at the end of the chapter.

Admirable as all these traits undoubtedly are, we cannot live up to them all the time. All human beings, including the most successful and competent, feel the full range of human emotions. The successful person does feel concern, can fear failure, senses rejection, is hurt by others, and at times even feels powerless and overwhelmed. The person who attempts to hide these stressful feelings sooner or later recognizes that they are still there, that the body is one place where they settle and reside, and that our behavior is the place where they are expressed.

If the "successful" person can experience these stresses, what about the "mature" person? Does maturity mean never experiencing the above concerns, fears, doubts, and hurts? I don't think so. Many people report that as they get older, some of their earlier doubts, fears, and hurts tend to diminish, if not disappear. However, with age (maturity), our lives do not become devoid of feelings; we are certainly not lacking in concerns. New fears, doubts, and hurts emerge, or perhaps they are just the old ones in new settings. If we define maturity as achieving that "blissful" state of experiencing only positive loving feelings, then maturity can easily evade many of us. Using this definition, I, for one, am not "mature." I used to think that eventually I could get there—to that state where I could handle everything well and, paradoxically, have few problems to handle. In fact, I expected that I'd gain a little each year and someday finally get there. I've been waiting a long time, and I haven't got there yet! Pretending I'm there when I'm really not, typically creates more stress for me, even more problems, and greater difficulties. I decided some time ago that being "immature" was perhaps a better state than lying. What about you?

There are other ideals or codes that we can use to guide our behavior instead of society's "mature," "successful," "calm executive," "cool," and "confident" ideals. These codes often originate from the spiritual and religious heritage of our society, but they evolve directly out of our own personal experience. We test these codes and ideals and modify them, forging them into our own personalized guide in times of stress. This approach to the development of a behavior code is well illustrated by Hans Selye. In his field of endeavor, Hans Selye is indeed a super-person. When I last heard the count of his accomplishments, he had written over thirty books and a thousand scientific articles and had received over nineteen honorary doctorates. He is a specialist in endocrinology and physiology, an M. D., and practically the inventor of the term "stress." I heard him speak several years ago. The talk was primarily on his personal solution to his own life stresses. Because of his research background, and because most of the audience were medical people, I expected his answer to involve some physiological solution. I was as surprised as was most of the audience by his answer. His personal solution to stress was not physiological or medical; it wasn't a drug or pill. It was a deeply personal solution, a slowly evolved one: It was simply a code for his behavior that he had developed over the years. This personal code was considered a basic aid in coping with lifelong stress (Selye, 1975).

How does a code of behavior help one in terms of stress? In times of stress, because our intellect is partially ineffectual, we often experience indecision, uncertainty, and emotional confusion. At times such as these, the code can tell us what to do and how to behave. It solves the confusion problem, gets us through the emotion or shock, and shows us the way to go. The code guides us at a time when we need guidance. Since the code is a self-imposed and self-developed one, the behavior guide that it offers should be realistic and acceptable to us. This is not always so when the guide is externally imposed.

What are some examples of codes of behavior that people develop for themselves and use as guides in terms of stress? Some illustrations follow:

To thine own self be true.
Be honest in dealing with others.

Never hurt another person.
Take time for self-nurturing.
Trust my own values, judgments, and ethics.
I don't always have to be the best or the first.
Ask, "Why am I doing this?"
Take time to communicate.
Consider the other guy and where he's coming from.
Some form of the Golden Rule: How would I want to be
    treated?

These are offered here merely to stimulate your own thinking. You can't use someone else's code. You have to do all the thinking about this. Your code is a highly personalized guide, perhaps more personal than any other approach offered in this book. It has to come deeply out of your own experience, out of what fits for you and makes sense for you. The above examples are not suggestions They are offered solely to help you begin to articulate your own ethical code more clearly. By clarifying your code—bringing it out in the open, as it were—it becomes more available to you. It becomes clearer, surer, and more useful. What basic principles guide your life? What is most important to you in making decisions dealing with stress? This code can contribute greatly to your self-discipline. Take the time to articulate it.

RECALL REMINDER

**A CODE
OF BEHAVIOR**

My own code of behavior includes such ideas as the following:

25

DIVERSIFY YOUR EMOTIONS

Diversify. The financial experts frequently recommend doing that regarding your income. Don't rely too heavily on just one source of income. Broaden your financial support. You are then in a stronger position if that single income source falters. You are then more able to cope with financial crises.

How about a similar recommendation regarding your emotional investments? Don't invest so heavily in work satisfaction that you neglect diversification. Invest your emotions in other activities of your life as well as your job. If you invest your emotions in a number of other activities in addition to your work, then if your work situation is stressed, you are more able to cope with those job difficulties.

Many individuals invest their emotions heavily in their work or in their families. They invest considerably less (or not at all) in other areas of life: friends, hobbies, sports, community, church, and the like.

Let's take a look at some of the traditional difficulties this can cause. First, we know what happens if a man invests too heavily just in his work. When he retires and loses his work, it can throw him fiercely. Statistics show that many men die relatively soon after retirement. Their emotional investments were concentrated solely in work to the neglect of other satisfactions. Next, remember the self-sacrificing mother who gives her "all" to her children. When the children get older, she won't let them grow up; she tries to hold on. She tries to get those same satisfactions as a mother, and this causes herself and her children much strife. This kind of mother seems to put all her emotions into her family. She has little or no real emotional interest in hobbies, friends, or community. Next, a personal example—that painful experience I mentioned earlier where my job, marriage, and family broke up all at once. At that time in my life, I had no emotions invested in friends, hobbies, and the like. My entire emotional world was centered on work and family. When both fell to pieces, I was completely thrown. I felt I had nothing, and I truly had nothing. I had not invested my emotions anywhere else.

Even on a weekly basis, if your job is especially stressful, isn't it nice to look forward to pleasurable friends, hobbies, church or community activities, and the like? During one particular week, if your job investment happens to arouse heavily negative feelings—disappointment, worry, or anger—other areas of your life that same week can add pleasurable emotions—enjoyment, uplifting, and esteem raising.

Many people invest heavily in job and in family. But on a weekly basis, there may be times when your family causes you stress or is going through an inevitable problem or crisis period. Sometimes, we rely too heavily on our families for support and pleasurable emotions (see Chapters 4 and 9). Again, spreading your emotions beyond the job/family to other areas of life might provide the advantages of diversification.

Let's take a look at how you are currently distributing your emotions. Look at Figure 25–1, which lists the typical

Areas of Investment	Estimate Current Investment	Future Diversification
Job		
Family		
Friends		
Hobbies		
Sports and physical Activities		
Community		
Church		
School		
Other?		
_____		
_____		
_____		
_____		
	100%	100%

Emotional Investment
Figure 25–1

areas of a person's life. Make a rough percentage estimate of how much you invest of your emotions (not your time) in job, family, and the like. Write these in the column labeled "Current Investment" (use a separate sheet if you would rather not write in the book). This is difficult to do, at best; so estimate only. Estimate very roughly: Round off, say, to 10 or 20 percent. Assign a percentage to work, then to family, and then to friends, going on down the column. Then check out your figures by adding them up: They must add up to 100 percent. If not, juggle them around. After it adds up to 100 percent, take a look at your distribution. Are you too concentrated in job, in family, or in both? Some people put 50 to 60 percent or more into their jobs and/or family.

Do you think it would help your stress level if you had

more emotional involvement in other areas of life? Can you see any value of spreading your emotions beyond the job? If so, do the chart again in the next column, "Future Diversification." If you are satisfied with your current distribution, don't, of course, bother. Otherwise, change the percentages. Lower the heavy ones; add to the ones you want to develop. Check again by adding up to 100 percent.

Many people, on redoing this, lower their job and family emotion (not time) to 40 or 30 percent or even less and decide to spread themselves in other areas.

If you decide to distribute your emotions, how do you proceed to do this? It's often difficult to lower emotions, that is, pull your emotions out from a job. Instead, most people find it easier to start making these changes by developing the areas they want to increase. Decide specifically what kind of activities would be enjoyable for you. For guidance in identifying new activities, you might find it helpful to consult the notes you made (the Recall Reminders) at the end of Chapter 13 or the Pleasurable Goodies; Chapter 18 on the Me-Act; Chapter 7 on Large Muscle Activity; Chapter 9 on Talking to Others; and Chapter 14 on Support Groups. Start by becoming involved in these new activities, and the enjoyment and closeness you begin developing in them will automatically diversify your emotions. You may very well find that, without attempting to reduce your emotions in your job/family, they have automatically lessened in response to your new satisfactions. Stress in the job has lost some of the significance it had in your total life picture.

Some people find that filling out the chart in Figure 25–1 is a very revealing experience. They had no idea they were putting all their eggs in one basket. They didn't realize that they had perhaps been slowly giving up other areas of their lives. Sometimes, we just don't realize how much our jobs have taken over our total lives. Check this one out for yourself.

RECALL REMINDER

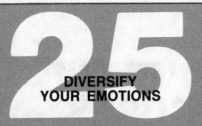

**DIVERSIFY
YOUR EMOTIONS**

I want to remember to increase my emotional investment
in the following areas:

26
COP-OUTS, EXCUSES, AND RATIONALIZATIONS

I don't have time (who does?).

It won't happen to me (it might not, but it probably will).

I don't have stress (return to page 1 and begin again).

My boss (subordinate, wife, husband, etc.) is my biggest problem (reread Chapter 8 on the Do-nut).

I don't get angry, annoyed, or tense (but have I checked with my secretary, spouse, or child?).

Things are going great (I should hope so!).

I don't have time (where are you going?).

I don't have time (for personal relationships?).

I've never been into physical exercise (remember what happened to the dinosaur?).

If I had a different job, I wouldn't have the stress (maybe, but does your neighbor's grass grow greener, too?).

I'm not athletic (neither am I).

I don't get angry often (just tense, tight, or cold).

If I could get rid of _____ , I wouldn't have stress (enjoy your fantasy and daydreaming).

I'm too busy (doing what?).

I'll start tomorrow (promises, promises).
List your own (please be convincing!). Now think of an
answer for each one!

_____

_____

_____

(Please Post)

RECALL REMINDER

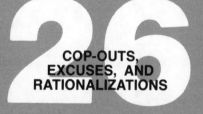

26

**COP-OUTS,
EXCUSES, AND
RATIONALIZATIONS**

Which cop-outs and excuses will I stop using? List
below.

V
PUTTING IT
ALL TOGETHER

27
RECALL AIDS

Since our memories operate poorly during stressful periods when alternatives are most needed, any aids to our memories will be valuable. Recall aids become even more significant when we are trying to make permanent changes in behavior that is ingrained, long-lasting, and habitual. These kinds of changes often require all the help we can get!

The Recall Reminders at the end of each chapter, which are summarized in the Appendix, have been developed for this purpose.* The reminders are your notes regarding specific techniques, approaches, and activities for you to use in the management of stress. Because they are your notes, you have individualized them to fit you. In each chapter, I suggest to the reader a number of possibilities that may be used by you, but you alone can decide which ones are truly for you. Your notes, therefore, are your own personalized summary of the book. If you haven't made notes while reading the book the first time around, you might want to flip through the chapters a second time. After read-

---

* If you haven't already done so, please refer to the Special Note to Readers.

ing a chapter, fill in your own notes on the Recall Reminder forms you copied from the Appendix.

Once you have developed these personalized notes, there are a number of different ways that you can use these Recall Reminders. Let's take a look at them.

ON A REGULARLY SCHEDULED BASIS

You may decide to refer to your notes at regular, scheduled times. Your scheduling of this depends on how often you want to be reminded of your stress level and the various techniques to handle stress. Your use of the scheduling method also depends somewhat on the particular calendar reminder system you currently use in your work. Some individuals use a daily folder system, one folder for each day of the week. They may then decide to keep their filled-in Recall Reminder, in, say, the Wednesday folder. Every Wednesday, when preparing for the day's work, they look through their recall notes, take the time to look at what's been happening that week, and do a quick assessment of their stress levels. Perhaps there is a need for looking at anger/dissatisfaction, or perhaps they've been neglectful of self-care, or whatever. Their Recall Reminder sheets then offer their individualized, specific ideas and techniques for action.

Some individuals set things up on a calendar basis. One person took his year's calendar and, on the first day of each month, wrote the word "stress." When that day arrives, he reaches in his files for his Recall Reminders. He then reviews what's been happening to his stress levels. Again, the review may force him to take the time to stop and self-monitor. This may result in, for example, recognition of unmet self-care needs or recalling of techniques not followed through on. You may want to use your calendar to refer you to your Recall Reminders.

THE AS NEEDED APPROACH

The second way that individuals can use their individual-ized notes is on an as needed basis. As you become more sensitive to your own stress indicators, you may find that you are monitoring yourself more frequently. You may well be able to sense your stress rising before it becomes too high. At any point in your emotional temperature, before you reach the peak, you can use your stress Recall Remind-ers to help you to avoid the heights. Your recall form then reminds you of a host of individualized techniques that work for you.

Or if you had a difficult experience, a rough few hours, a tough day, or a bad week, pull out your reminder notes and recall what you can do about it. I use my notes this way. Even though I have developed these Recall Reminders my-self, I don't have them on my mind all the time. I, too, need to be reminded. After a trying experience, I look through my notes, recall that perhaps I haven't had much solitude lately or that I have some Me-Acts on my list that I haven't en-joyed lately. Or perhaps I am reminded to use the Do-nut further to understand my anger/dissatisfaction even better, or perhaps I realize that I've been neglecting some other important need. You might, of course, combine this "as needed" approach with a regular, scheduled stress check-up—say, once a week or once a month.

MAKE A CONTRACT WITH YOURSELF

You may decide to make a contract with yourself to help you feel more sense of commitment to your stress goals. This is still another way to work toward specific goals that you have set for your stress management. One easy way to do this is to refer again to your personalized Recall Re-minder sheets. Or go through the book, chapter by chapter. As a specific item seems relevant to you, write down, on a separate contract form, the specific goals that you want to achieve. For example, "I want to deal with anger toward my boss by using the Do-nut," or "I want to start a regular daily LMA program by bicycling," or "I want to distribute my emotions more widely by developing friends." State these as "I wants" or, better yet, as "I wills." Write them on a separate, dated, contract form. Set a date, too, for achieving each of these goals. It might also help to list the specific steps necessary to achieve each goal—for example, "I will fix the flat tire on my bicycle next Saturday" (a necessary step before I can start using the bike for LMA), or "I will call Jack tomorrow to have lunch together" (specifically to develop a friendship with him). If this kind of specificity is too much for you, don't tie yourself up so tight that it will turn you off to the whole process. Do what is necessary to get you started toward change. Perhaps just listing your "I wills" is sufficient. At the least, however, do write in a date on your contract to accomplish each "I will." Do this so that you can check out the contract to see if you have achieved your specific goals. Some people like to sign their names at the bottom of the contract to add more feeling of intention and dedication.

Sometimes a joint contract with a spouse or partner adds the necessary social support we often need. For example, "We will, every morning, before breakfast, walk/jog together for twenty minutes." This may well keep it going for you. Consider joint contracts.

SIGNS, POSTERS, AND OTHER GRAPHIC REMINDERS

Some individuals tend spontaneously to develop graphic means of helping them recall what they want to remember. To be reminded of the recall items, some people actually post their entire Recall Reminder list on a bulletin board, on their bathroom mirror, or on the refrigerator door. Or you might prefer to select specific items for graphic display.

Some persons use 3″ × 5″ cards and list reminder items on them. Or take your contract list and print each "I will" on a 3″ × 5″ card. Carry these cards in your jacket or attaché case, or place them in your center desk drawer.

You might make up specific signs with a broad felt pen on an 8½ × 11″ sheet and post these at relevant places at work or home where you will notice them or trip over them (see Figure 27–1). Make up your own designs or your own slogans. This can be fun and creative. Some people who are dedicated to dealing with anger/dissatisfaction differently

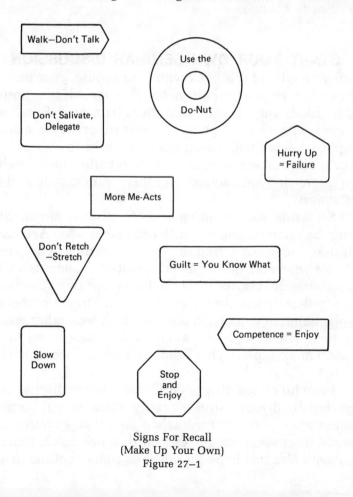

Signs For Recall
(Make Up Your Own)
Figure 27–1

have actually baked donuts to remind them of you know what, made clay donut-shaped jewelry to hang around their necks or used bagels or life savers—all to remind them of the alternatives in dealing with anger. One individual bought a number of small plastic toy shovels (about five to six inches long), painted the blades a messy brown color, and called them "shit shovels"—to remind her of what to do with her guilt. It doesn't take much artistic talent, but the possibilities are endless. The results are reminders (and often humorous ones) of how we want to behave and of how we want to change.

START YOUR OWN SEMINAR DISCUSSION

Share a chapter of this book with your spouse, your partner, a coworker, or your subordinates. Discuss self-monitoring, anger, LMA, Me-Acts, or solitude. Share your Recall Reminders with another person. If you supervise or manage people, sit down with them, individually or in a group, and discuss relevant stress issues that might affect their productivity, their job satisfaction, and their team morale and cohesiveness.

Set aside staff meeting time to discuss stress. Start using the same vocabulary with each other—Me-Act, LMA, solitude, and so on. Using these same words will help each to know where the other guy is at, will ease communication during stressful periods, and can foster more effective working together. Often after using the same stress vocabulary, an office staff or work team will joke with each other regarding their stress, and that alone will release some of the stress. For example, "That deadline's gonna force me into a Me-Act."

Have lunch together once a week—not to discuss business but to discuss stress. Set up more formal seminar discussions—perhaps a workshop on stress, a course, or a weekly discussion group. Use work time, lunch time, or whatever. Use this book for a text or course outline. If you feel that you need a leader, reach out to your company training department, to your company psychologist, or to other resources in your organization. If none are available, have each group member choose one chapter of the book that particularly interests him or her and lead the weekly discussion on that chapter. After your seminar or discussion group is over, set up follow-up sessions to support changes and to check up on changes. Support each other, help each other, and lean on each other. Discuss, for example, how you can use venting with each other (Chapter 9) or where you can develop a solitude place in your building.

OTHER SOURCES OF SUPPORT AND RECALL

Invite spouses or partners to attend professional (or vocational) yearly conventions where the topic of stress is discussed.

At monthly meetings of whatever vocational organization you belong to, have the topic of stress placed on the program.

Recommend a two-day seminar or workshop on stress to be held in some beautiful retreat setting away from work. Develop this retreat seminar for your work group, management team, or staff group.

Use journal writing to explore your own attitudes, feelings, and responses to any stress topic. Share your journals with spouses, partners, and coworkers.

In summary, many of us find that self-discipline can be reinforced by verbal contact with others—by discussions with spouses and coworkers, by regular meetings or courses, and so on. Self-discipline can also be reinforced by scheduling—regular stress check-ups and regular times set aside to self-monitor, to try out approaches, and to evaluate them. Self-discipline rarely occurs spontaneously. It requires some form of commitment and some time spent on following through on the commitment. Choose your own recall approach, the one that works best for you.

RECALL REMINDER

27

RECALL AIDS

Take a few minutes to consider how you are going to use the material in this book.

_____I will use the Recall Reminders regularly. Make a

note on my calendar every week_____,

month_____, and so on.

_____I will make a personal contract with myself describing specific changes I want to make.

_____I want to make graphic aids, signs, posters, and so on to remind me.

_____Other ways? What? Make a note.

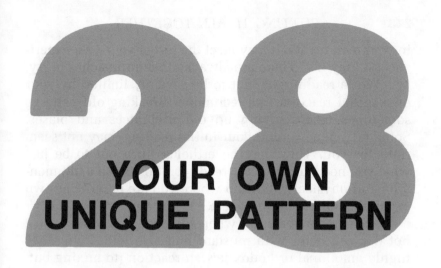

YOUR OWN UNIQUE PATTERN

You've been exposed in this book to many and diverse ideas, suggestions, and techniques. It's your job now to make sense out of it and to fit it in to your unique Self. The pattern you develop must agree with you; it must match your experience. The result will be a highly personalized view of stress and a thoroughly individualized range of techniques for coping with stress.

Every one of us is radically different. The eccentricity of our thoughts and experiences powerfully affects what we are. In some ways, this individuality is our greatest asset in what we bring to our work and to our total life. Our uniqueness means, above all, that a technique that works admirably for someone else may not work at all for you. No one technique can be for everyone. That's the major reason why this stress book offers so many different approaches. Somewhere in all this is something for you. It is doubtful that anyone else understands you well enough to be able to ferret out just what is right for you. You must do this for yourself.

Check out each chapter in turn. Try it out on your mind first, and see how it fits. If it seems to make sense, test it out in your own reality. It may meet the test of your own experience; it may not. There are always other approaches to try.

While reading, try not to be severely limited by your own initial reaction to a technique. Breaking old patterns sometimes means giving up old prejudices and biases. Some techniques, upon your initial reading, may not seem right for you. They may nevertheless turn out to be just what you need and are now ready for. So stretch a bit, mentally and physically, beyond where you are now. Your own experience is the ultimate test.

I remember years ago when someone first offered me a hot dog on a bun with mustard and also with butter. My highly emotional orthodox Jewish reaction (to mixing butter and meat) was strongly negative—until the first bite. It was delicious. It's the only way I've eaten hot dogs since. Give your own experience the chance.

Try combining techniques. For example, use LMA to quiet you down enough to then use a Me-Act or Progressive Relaxation. Mix these techniques any way you like. You might want to vary the mix (doing a different form of LMA each day). Or you may prefer to stay persistently with one set of approaches in order to develop a regularity or pattern.

Remember that change is a basic ingredient of life. This is particularly so in our highly stressful times. What works for you now might not continue to be effective in the future. After a company reorganization six months from now, when you get a new boss, when the market or the neighborhood changes, when you change jobs, when you retire, or when the world moves on to a different place: Any of these might require different stress approaches. Re-evaluate your management of stress at crucial times in your life. Be open to different ways of looking at your stress; be open to new approaches.

I end this book with feelings toward you, the unknown reader: feelings of care and concern, a hope that I have been of some help, and my best wishes for at least a somewhat less stressful future.

RECALL REMINDER

**YOUR OWN
UNIQUE PATTERN**

Check, if appropriate, the following:

_____I want to take the time to develop a unique, personalized plan for stress management.

_____Any changes recently in my life/work that might require new techniques or a new look at my total plan?

Epilogue

If I am not for myself,
    Who will be for me?
If I am not for others,
    What am I?
If not now,
    When?

                The *Talmud*

APPENDIX

RECALL REMINDERS

RECALL REMINDER

1. *Aching Bodies*
List the places where stress comes out in my body:

_____

2. *Unreasonable Behavior*
I want to avoid the following high stress, unreasona-

ble, irrational, nonproductive behaviors:_____

_____

3. *Anger*
I want to stop putting down: Who?

_____

_____

Numbers correspond with Chapter numbers

4. *Dumping On My Family*
I want to stop taking out my anger/dissatisfaction on:

_____

5. *Self-monitoring*
In a recent stress episode:

My behaviors:_____

My body signals:_____

My feelings:_____

6. *Don't Rely On Your Feelings*
I want to get more input on how I behave from:

_____

7. *LMA*
At work, what can I do physically:

_____

What kind of LMA do I or can I use regularly:

_____

8. *Do-Nut*
My underlying hurt feelings are:

_____

_____

Numbers correspond with Chapter numbers

9. *Talking to Others*

I should talk more to:_____

_____

10. *Slow Down*
I want to slow down while doing the following: (and see the possible effects):

_____

11. *Crises and Emergencies*
I want to try to:

Schedule?_____

Prioritize, screen?_____

Use Five-Year Rule?_____

12. *Muscle Relaxation*

Progressive Relaxation_____

Yoga_____

Massage_____

Meditation_____

Biofeedback_____

Self-hypnosis_____

Numbers correspond with Chapter numbers

13. *Pleasurable Goodies*

Music_____ Rituals_____

Laughter_____ Buying_____

Poetry_____ Play_____

Apologizing to_____ Rest_____

Hug—who?_____ Hot bath_____

Cry_____ When to begin?_____

14. *Support Groups*
Join or attend more regularly:

_____

Develop closeness—how?_____

_____

15. *Human Pain*
Defusing techniques—which ones?

_____

Learning from hurt—what?_____

_____

Changing my attitude_____

Numbers correspond with Chapter numbers

16. *Guilt*
Recall the psychological definition of guilt—when?

_____

17. *Solitude*

When and where during the day or night?_____

18. *Me-Act*
List browsing, loafing, puttering, wandering Me-Acts

_____

_____

19. *Physical Health*

Reduce "baddies":_____

_____

Reduce heart attack risks:_____

_____

20. *Competition*

I want to reduce my competition—where?_____

_____

Numbers correspond with Chapter numbers

21. Sex
Begin regular, routine LMA—when:

_____

Develop closeness and body release in sex—how?

_____

22. *Personal Strengths*

Positive statement list?_____

Positive trait list?_____

Other sources of strength?_____

_____

Develop flexibility and learning—how?_____

_____

23. *Stop Indulging Feelings*
I will give in less often to the following feelings:

_____

_____

Inner motivations:_____

_____

Numbers correspond with Chapter numbers

24. *Code*

My code includes:_____

_____

_____

25. *Diversify Emotions*

I will increase my emotional investment in:_____

_____

_____

26. *Cop-Outs*
I will avoid the following cop-outs or excuses:_____

_____

_____

27. *Recall Aids*
I will reread these Recall Reminders how frequently:

_____

I need more graphic aids to remind me of_____

_____

I last checked my personal contract when?_____

_____

Numbers correspond with Chapter numbers

28. *Re-Evaluation*
I want to make a personalized plan

_____

I need to re-assess my plan because of life/work

changes_____

Epilogue

If not, now—when?_____

_____

REFERENCES CITED IN THE TEXT

Arieti, Silvano, Ed. *American Handbook of Psychiatry.* New York: Basic Books, 1975.

Bart, Charles H., and Taylor, N. B. *A Textbook in Human Physiology,* 4th ed. New York: Holt, Rinehart & Winston, 1958.

Belloc, Nedra B. "Relationship of Health Practices & Mortality." *Preventative Medicine* 2 (1973), 67–81.

Benson, Herbert. *The Relaxation Response.* New York: Morrow, 1975.

Bernhardt, Roger, and Martin, David. *Self-Mastery Through Self Hypnosis.* Indianapolis: Bobbs-Merrill, 1977.

Brady, J. V., and others. "Avoidance Behavior and the Development of Gastrointestinal Ulcers." *Journal of the Experimental Analysis of Behavior* 1 (1958), 69–73.

Brown, Barbara. *Stress and the Art of Biofeedback.* New York: Harper & Row, Pub., 1977.

Carruthers, Malcolm. *The Western Way of Death.* New York: Pantheon Books, 1974.

Cofer, C. N., and Appley, M. H. *Motivation Theory and Research.* New York: John Wiley, 1964.

Cousins, Norman. "Anatomy of an Illness." *Saturday Review,* May 28, 1977.

Crom, Scott. *Quaker Worship and Techniques of Meditation.* Pendle Hill Pamphlet, 1974.

Downing, George. *The Massage Book.* New York: Random House, 1972.

Fixx, James F. *The Complete Book of Running.* New York: Random House, 1977.

Glasser, William. *Positive Addiction.* New York: Harper & Row, 1976.

Goleman, David. *The Varieties of Meditative Experience.* New York: Dutton, 1977.

Gordon, Thomas. *P.E.T., Parent Effectiveness Training.* New York: Peter H. Wyden, 1970.

Higdon, Hal. *Fitness After Forty.* Mt. View, Cal.: World Publications, 1977.

Hilgard, E. R., Atkinson, Richard, and Atkinson, Rita. *Introduc-*

tion to Psychology. New York: Harcourt Brace Jovanovich, 1975.

Jansen, G. *Noise As a Cause of Disease.* Army Foreign Science and Technology Center, Report No. FSTC–HT–23–241–71, 1971.

LaMaze, Fernand. *Painless Childbirth.* Chicago: Henry Regnery, 1970.

LeShan, Lawrence. *How to Meditate, A Guide to Self Discovery.* Boston: Little, Brown, 1974.

Moody, Raymond A. *Laugh After Laugh–The Healing Power of Humor.* Jacksonville, Fla.: Headwater Press, 1978.

Orlick, Terry. *The Cooperative Sports and Games Book—Challenge Without Competition.* New York: Pantheon, 1978.

Rahe, Richard H., and Arthur, R. D. *Journal of Human Stress* 4 (1978), 3–15.

Rosenman, Ray, and Friedman, Meyer. *Type A Behavior and Your Heart.* New York: Knopf, 1974.

Rowland, Kay F., and Sokol, Bernice. "A Review of Research Examining the Coronary Prone Behavior Pattern." *Journal of Human Stress* 3 (1977), 26–33.

Selye, Hans. *Stress Without Distress.* New York: NAL, 1975.

Shaffer, L. T. "Fear and Courage in Aerial Combat." *Journal of Consulting Psychology* 11 (1947), 139.

Smith, Manuel J. *When I Say No, I Feel Guilty.* New York: Bantam, 1975.

Syme, S. Leonard. "Social and Psychological Risk Factors in Coronary Heart Disease." *Modern Concepts of Cardiovascular Disease* 64 (1975), 4, American Heart Association.

Thomas, Lewis. *The Lives of a Cell—Notes of a Biology Watcher.* New York: Bantam, 1974.

Wallace, Robert Keith, and Benson, Herbert. (1972) *Scientific American,* 2/72:84–90.

Weiss, J. M. (1972) "Psychological Factors in Stress and Disease." *Scientific American,* 226:106. 7

Yogi, Maharishi Mahesh. *Transcendental Meditation, Serenity Without Drugs.* New York: Signet, 1968.

FURTHER READING

Part 1—Telling It Like It Is

Brown, Barbara. *Stress and the Art of Biofeedback.* New York:

Harper & Row, Pub., 1977. Just exactly why our muscles behave the way they do while we are experiencing stress is far from clear. This book (pp. 26–50) is an excellent explanation of what is currently known about the physiology of that complicated process.

Carruthers, Malcolm. *The Western Way of Death.* New York: Pantheon, 1974. Carruthers, an English pathologist, describes his research on stress effects of driving a car, giving a public speech, and other situations. Very uncomfortable reading, especially for car-crazed Americans!

Layden, Milton. *Escaping the Hostility Trap.* Englewood Cliffs, N.J.: Prentice-Hall, 1977. Read this discussion of all the negative effects of anger—on pilots, air controllers, blacks, all of us.

Rahe, Richard, H., and Arthur, R. D. (1978) *Journal of Human Stress,* vol. 4:3–15. This is probably the most recent and thorough summary of life change studies.

Rosenman, Ray and Friedman, Meyer *Type A Behavior and Your Heart.* New York: Knopf, 1974. This is the book referred to in the Preface. Read it to discover your own coronary-prone traits.

Wall Street Journal, April 2–10, 1979. A series of four articles summarizing recent proof that "research is indicating that stress is linked to physical illness."

Part 2—Breaking the Pattern

Benson, Herbert. *The Relaxation Response.* New York: Morrow, 1975. A simple, relatively straightforward approach to meditation with much medical supportive data.

Brenton, Myron. *Friendship.* Briarcliff Manor, N.Y.: Stein & Day, 1974. One of the few studies of friendship.

Cousins, Norman. "Anatomy of an Illness." *Saturday Review,* May 28, 1977. This is Norman Cousins' own description of his use of humor (and massive doses of vitamin C) in curing his own illness.

Downing, George. *The Massage Book.* New York: Random House, 1972. An excellent introduction to massage.

Feitis, Rosemary, (Ed.,) *Ida Rolf Talks About Rolfing & Physical Reality.* New York: Harper & Row, Pub., 1978.

Fixx, James F. *The Complete Book of Running.* New York: Random House, 1977. So much has been written about the value of physical exercise on our emotions that you can pick almost any sport and find material describing this. Read this book as an example.

Folan, Lillias M. *Lillias, Yoga and You.* Cincinnati, Ohio: WCET–TV This paperback is available from your local PBS TV station.

Frankl, Viktor E. *Man's Search for Meaning, An Introduction to Logo-therapy.* New York: Pocket Books, 1963. Frankl has written much on his experience and its application to psychotherapy. This is an easy one to start with.

Glasser, William. *Positive Addiction.* New York: Harper & Row, Pub., 1976. The book describes meditation as a positive addiction state (see Chapter 22).

Goleman, David. *The Varieties of Meditative Experience.* New York: Dutton, 1977. The religious, historical, and philosophical background of meditation in detail.

Gordon, Thomas. *P.E.T., Parent Effectiveness Training.* New York: Peter H. Wyden, 1970. This is one of many self-help books that will train you in how to listen more effectively.

Greenberg, Herbert M. *Teaching With Feeling,* New York: Macmillan, 1969.

Jacobson, Edmund. *You Must Relax.* 5th ed. New York: McGraw-Hill, 1970. One of many books by Jacobson describing his approach to Progressive Relaxation.

LeShan, Lawrence. *How to Meditate, a Guide to Self-Discovery.* Boston: Little, Brown, 1974. This is a classic. Excellent for self-instruction.

Lindemann, Hannes. (1973) *Relieve Tension the Autogenic Way.* New York: Peter H. Wyden, 1973.

Miller, Emmett E. *Feeling Good—How to Stay Healthy.* Englewood Cliffs, N.J.: Prentice-Hall, 1978.

Miller, Roberta DeLong. *Psychic Massage.* New York: Harper & Row, Pub., 1975.

Mindess, Harvey. *Laughter After Liberation, Developing Your Sense of Humor, The Psychology of Laughter.* Los Angeles, Cal.: Nash Publishing, 1971. This book offers specific help in developing your sense of humor, mainly by pointing out attitudes that interfere with our humor.

Moody, Raymond A. *Laugh After Laugh—The Healing Power of Humor.* Jacksonville, Fla.: Headwater Press, 1978. A new look at the old use of humor for healing. History plus a medical point of view.

Rawls, Eugene S., and Diskin, Eve. *Yoga for Beauty and Health.* West Nyack, N.Y.: Parker Publishing Co., 1967.

de Saint-Exupery, Antoine *The Little Prince.* Harcourt Brace Jovanovich, 1943. A classic, beautiful tale of closeness. Re-read it.

Weinstock, Marya. *The Extended Family Program Reconsidered—Seven Years Later.* Mimeographed, 1978. Available from the Unitarian Church, 1535 Santa Barbara St., Santa Barbara, Cal. 93101

Yee, Min ,S., and Wright, Donald K. *The Great Escape—A Source Book of Delights and Pleasures for the Mind and Body.* New York: Bantam, 1974. A little bit of everything is in here— Belly Dancing, Rafting, Rolfing, Houseboats, Hang-gliding, Ballooning, and so on. A wild conglomeration!

Part 3—Taking Care of Yourself

Comfort, Alex, Ed. *More Joy of Sex—A Love-Making Companion to The Joy of Sex.* New York: Simon & Schuster, 1974. Detailed description of how to involve your entire body and senses in love-making—for heightened joy and release.

Cooper, Kenneth. *The New Aerobics.* New York: Bantam, 1975. Cooper's books are the classics in aerobic (cardiovascular) exercise. His methods use charts for each sport (running, swimming, etc.) and quantify the aerobic value for each time/distance. He and his wife have developed charts for women, too.

Higdon, Hal. *Fitness After Forty.* Mt. View, Cal.: World Publications, 1977. Excellent fitness book for all ages. See especially Chapter 7, "Death of a Distance Runner," for some discussion of competition and running.

Kavanaugh, Terence. *Heart Attack? Counter-Attack!* New York: Van Nostrand Reinhold, 1976. Would you believe that men who have had two heart attacks have completed the Boston Marathon? Read it by the physician who trained them. Exercise again.

Orlick, Terry. *The Cooperative Sports and Games Book—Challenge Without Competition.* New York: Pantheon, 1978. Fascinating, vigorous, and noncompetitive! This is the best of the New Games books. Some of them sneak competition in, and this one does not.

Rudner, Ruth. *Forgotten Pleasures—A Guide for the Seasoned Adventurer.* New York: Viking, 1978. Description of basically tary adventures: walking in the woods, skipping stones, berrying, night sounds and scents, and so on. Neat joys that are easily available to us.

Smith, Manuel J. *When I Say No, I Feel Guilty.* New York: Bantam, 1975. Specific techniques for becoming more assertive, including dealing with your boss.

Thomas, Lewis. *The Lives of a Cell—Notes of a Biology Watcher.* New York: Bantam, 1974.

Zohman, Lenore R. *Beyond Diet—Exercise Your Way to Fitness and Heart Health.* A pamphlet available for fifteen cents from Mazola Nutrition Information Service, Box 307, Coventry, Connecticut 06238. Excellent description of cardiovascular exercise using the conventional pulse-count method. Good detail on choosing exercises and on recognizing negative symptoms.

Part 4—Our Strengths

Selye, Hans. *Stress Without Distress.* New York: NAL, 1975.

INDEX

anger, 23–33
  indirect, 31–2
  reducing, 78–88
  situations, 25–7
angry people, dealing with 86–7
apologies, 130–2
assertiveness, 159–60
attitude, 150–51

B

baddies, The 184–5
behavior vs. feelings, 220–21
bicycling, 189
biofeedback, 119–20
blood:
  coagulation, 75–6
  pressure, 72–3
body, stress reactions of 7–15
browsing, 175

C

catharsis, 89
challenge, 190–1

changing oneself (Section IV),
  205–235
closeness activities, 142–44
code of behavior, 223–228
coffee breaks, 157, 166
compassion, 85, 93
competition, 178, 189–196
  job, 192
  sneaky, 191
  sports, 193
confrontation, 84–86
contract, to aid committment
  241–242
cop-outs, 234–5
Cousins, Norman, 128
crises & emergencies, 106–113
crying, 133–4

D

deadlines, 156
defusing painful emotions, 147
dependency, 207–8
digestive system & stress, 74–75
dissatisfaction, 25–27

diversify emotions, 229–233
Do-nut, 78–88, 146, 148
driving a car, 27, 52–3, 82
duty & responsibility, 215–17

E

emotional temperature, 17, 20–21
emotions, (see feelings)
Epilogue, 250
excuses, 234–5
exercise, 66–71

F

feelings, 51–57
   diversify, 229–233
   indulging, 214–22
   painful, 79–80
Fight or Flight reaction, 64
Five-Year Rule, 112–13
flexibility, 210–11
Frankl, Viktor 149–51

G

Glasser, William 208–9
goals, 177–178
guilt, 155–60, 178

H

hate, sharing 90
health, physical (including diet,
   nutrition, longevity),
   182–88
heart disease, 9–12; 49; 53
   reducing risk of, 185–87
heart rate, 73
hidden agenda, 31–32
hot tubs, 138
hugging & touch, 132–33
humour, 128–29
hypnosis, 123–24

I

illness, 8–15
imagery, 123–24
integration, racial 220
interruptions, 106–7
irrational behavior, 18–22
isolation, 162
isometrics, 68

J

Jacobson, Edmund 116

L

Large Muscle Activity (LMA),
   61–77, 83, 197–202
LeShan, Lawrence 122
life changes, 9–10
listeners, 92, 94
listening, 90
loafing, 174
longevity, 184
loneliness, 167
love, 195
loved ones, 35–6

M

managers, 25–6, 81, 106–7, 139,
   224
massage, 117–19
maturity, 225
Me-Act, 171–80
medical exam, 200
meditation, 120–22
men, sharing feelings, 92–93
mini-failures, 99
mini-slowdowns, 103–4
mini-vacations, 172–80
moderation, 183–4
muscles, 12–13, 61–77, 114–125
music, 127–8

N

New Games, 194
noise, 52
non-competitive behavior, 195

O

Orlick, Terry and the New
    Games, 194

P

pain, 146−52
  learning from, 147−8
parents, 81−82, 26, 35−6
personalizing techniques, 247−49
play, 137, 176
pleasurable goodies, 126−39
plural activities, 97, 103
poetry, 129−30
Positive:
  addiction, 208−9
  commendation file, 205−6
  trait list, 206−7
prayer & worship, 130
productivity & stress 18−19,
    100−102, 159, 177,
  job criteria, 207−8
Progressive Relaxation, 116−17
prioritizing, 109−12
psychosomatic, 8, 182−83
punishment & self-discipline,
    218−19
put-downs, 28−30
puttering, 175−6

R

Re-Act, 172
Recall Aids, 239−46
    Reminders, see at end of
    each chapter, appendix, &
    Special Note to Reader

relaxation methods, 114−25
religion, 130, 135, 136
renewal, 157, 163, 177
rituals, traditions, & routine,
    134−36
Rolfing, 118
rushing, 98−100

S

scheduling, 108−9, 179
  and recall aids, 240−41
self-care, 155−202
self-discipline, 214−222
self esteem, 136
self-monitoring, 39−50
  input, 54−55, 180
  steps, 42−49
Selye, Hans 226
sex, 197−202
signs & posters for recall aid,
    242−43
single parents, 177
sleep, 138−9
slowing down, 97−105
small muscle activity, 68−69
solitude, 161−69
  lounges, 161
spending money, 136
sports, (see LMA), 193
strengths, personal 205−213
stress:
  contract with oneself, 241
  decision, 48−49
  good, 43−45
  high, 46−48
  increasing, 29−33
  levels, 43
  low to moderate, 44−45
  lowering, 9, 62, 64
  personalizing, 247−8
  physiological changes, 63−64,
    72−76
  seminars at work, 244−45

stress (cont.)
  transfer, 35–38
stressors, 172
super-persons, in society 223–24
support groups, 142–45; 245

T

thinking:
  kinds required, 164–5
  loss of ability, 16–22
  on job, 163–64
time management, 156, 159,
    165–7; 179
Type A (see Heart Disease)
  and competitiveness, 193
  LMA, 200–201

U

unreasonable behaviors, 16–22

V

venting Stress, 89–96
Vocational Placement Formula,
    110–11

W

walking, 65–66, 173
wet feet syndrome, 107–8
women, special problems 158, 177
work ethic, 155–60

Y

Yoga, 117

□ Please charge my □ MasterCard □ Visa

Credit Card # _____ Exp. date _____

Signature _____

□ Enclosed is my check or money order.
*Publisher pays postage and handling charges
for prepaid and charge card orders.

□ Bill me.

Name _____ Apt. # _____

Address _____

City/State _____ Zip _____

MERCHANDISE TOTAL		
ADD:	SALES TAX FOR YOUR STATE	
	*12% POSTAGE AND HANDLING	
TOTAL: CHECK ENCLOSED		

PLEASE ALLOW FOUR WEEKS FOR DELIVERY

Send your order to:
Prentice Hall Press Mail Order Billing
Route 59 at Brook Hill Drive
West Nyack, NY 10994

Phone (201) 767-5937 for
any additional ordering
information.